MW01092108

BUNS

BUNS

Sweet and
Simple Bakes

LOUISE HURST

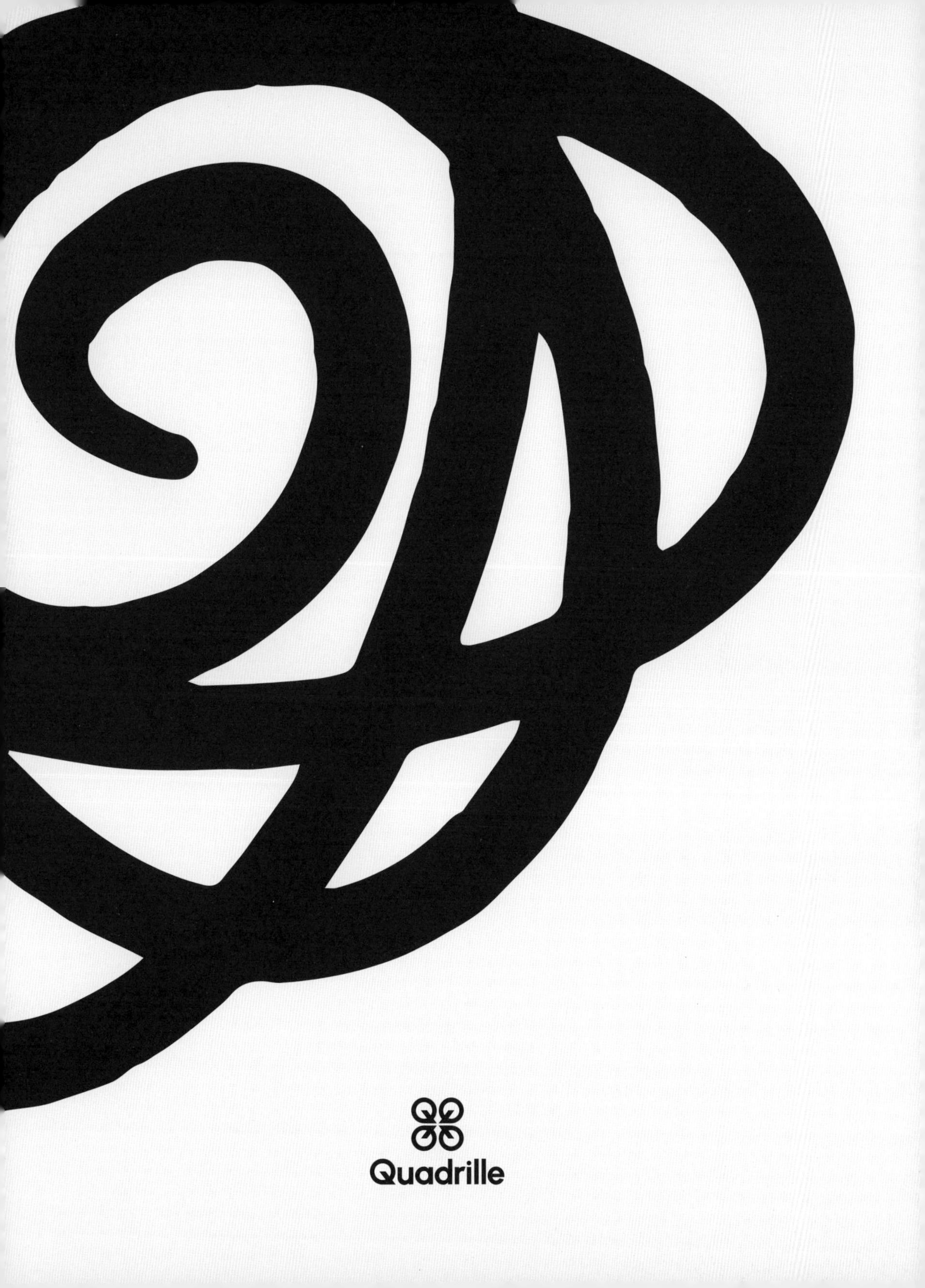
Quadrille

CONTENTS

INTRODUCTION

There is something universally comforting about a freshly baked bun. Soft and pillowy, with a gentle sweetness and enticing aroma, they are a treat enjoyed by cultures around the globe. From the bustling bakeries of Sweden to the cozy kitchens of Italy and the vibrant marketplaces of Poland, buns are a testament to the universal appeal of simple, sweet indulgence. At the heart of this global love affair is the basic pleasure of taking a few ingredients and transforming them into something truly delicious.

One of the most remarkable aspects of enriched yeasted buns is their widespread popularity. Despite vast differences in culinary traditions and ingredients, nearly every culture has its own version. In Sweden, for instance, *kanelbullar*, or cinnamon buns, are a national treasure, enjoyed with a coffee during a fika (break). The classic Swedish version is typically filled with cinnamon, sugar and butter, rolled into a spiral and topped with sugar nibs, giving it a distinctive look and flavour.

In Italy, *maritozzi* are a Roman specialty: sweet buns split and filled with lightly whipped cream, making them a decadent breakfast or dessert. Meanwhile, in Poland, *drożdżówki* are soft buns often filled with fruit preserves and/or sweet cheese, and are a favourite among children and adults alike.

The enduring popularity of sweet buns can be attributed to several factors. Firstly, the basic ingredients required to make them are simple and readily available: flour, sugar, yeast, butter and eggs. These larder staples form the foundation of countless recipes, allowing for endless variations and adaptations. Secondly, the active time required to prepare them is relatively minimal. While the dough needs time to rise, the hands-on process is straightforward and methodical, making it an accessible project for both novice and experienced bakers alike.

Lastly, there is something inherently rewarding about the process of making buns. The rhythmic kneading of the dough, the anticipation as it rises, and the intoxicating aroma that fills the kitchen as the buns bake all contribute to a deeply satisfying experience. Once you get the hang of it, baking sweet yeasted buns can become a mindful ritual – a way to connect with culinary traditions from around the world while creating something delicious to share with family and friends.

In this book, we will explore the diverse world of buns, from traditional recipes passed down through generations to modern interpretations that push the boundaries of flavour and form. Whether you are a seasoned baker or a curious beginner, this journey will inspire you to create your own delicious bakes, celebrate the rich tapestry of global culinary traditions, and perhaps even discover new favourites along the way.

ABOUT THE AUTHOR

I have spent my whole life in kitchens. My earliest food memory is when I was about five years old, baking cinnamon buns with my *mormor* (Swedish grandmother). In the midst of chaos, I managed to create delicious, fluffy, golden swirls showered in crunchy sugar nibs. It was then that I discovered how creative baking could be.

Many of my favourite bakes came from my grandmother, who helped devise recipes for her local village bakery in Äppleviken. My Swedish heritage has influenced my entire cooking career.

At 18, I began my professional training, culminating in a diploma from Leith's School of Food and Wine. I then worked in several restaurants, honing my skills in order to embark on my ultimate ambition to be a private chef.

I loved bringing together interesting flavours for catering jobs – it was always exciting and a little nerve-racking. I would come back to the kitchen from foreign holidays with ideas from the artisan markets of Denmark, France and Italy and would test new recipes inspired by the local ingredients.

I've been greatly influenced by my heritage, and trips abroad. Whenever I travel now, I make notes and research in advance to find the best local spots for eating, drinking coffee and buying sourdough bread and pastries. I seek out dishes I've seen online and speak with locals about their best-loved recipes. One of my favourites is an orange and fennel cake, a recipe given to me by a lady we stayed with in Sicily, which inspired the use of fennel in my Maritozzi recipe (see pages 111–12).

In recent years, I've thoroughly enjoyed making sourdough rye bread and cinnamon and cardamom buns for my local farmers' market. Chatting to customers, I discovered their enthusiasm to produce their own bakes and many would ask me about ingredients, timings and techniques. This led me to host baking workshops geared towards people's different skill levels, from making simple cardamom buns to sourdough from scratch.

I started a food blog in 2017 and quickly gained loyal followers. Initially, it was to showcase my Scandinavian-influenced recipes. I'm still answering questions about ingredients, timings, and techniques – many of which are addressed in these pages.

In this book, you'll find my approach to baking, a little bit of science, but most importantly, joy. As you explore the pages, you'll discover my favourite ingredients, inspired by childhood memories and places I've visited. Baking with yeast might seem like a daunting task, but I will take you through each step. It's actually very rewarding once you get the hang of it. From blending the ingredients to kneading the dough to knowing when it's fully proved and ready to bake, I'll break down each process, share some useful tips, and show you how to take the guesswork out of working with yeast.

Food has always played a significant role in my life and I am as obsessed with cooking today as I was when I first tasted the buns I baked with my *mormor*. Discovering the ability to cook is very special. I want to inspire you to get into your kitchen and find out how amazing baking can be.

I'd like to add that no buns were wasted in the making of this book. The local homeless drop-in centre, my neighbours and my family were all extremely grateful recipients.

Louise

INGREDIENTS

Baking buns at home doesn't require a larder full of specialty ingredients. With a few good-quality staples, you can create simple yet delicious bakes. Here are the basic ingredients you'll need, showing how a thoughtful selection can elevate your baking. From organic flour to fresh spices, each component plays a vital role in achieving the perfect texture and flavour in your homemade buns.

BUTTER

Butter plays a crucial role in sweet yeasted buns, enhancing both flavour and texture. High-quality butter has a greater fat content, which means it contains less water. Opting for unsalted butter allows you to adjust seasoning to suit your taste preferences.

CHOCOLATE

In baked goods, a good-quality chocolate will reflect in the end result. I'm a fan of the Belgian brand Callebaut, and I consistently use good-quality dark chocolate with 54% cocoa solids. I don't use baking chocolate; it contains additives and artificial flavourings that I don't wish to consume.

EGGS

Use organic free-range eggs, or the best you can find. Typically, I buy large eggs, although size doesn't really matter, as I always weigh the cracked egg for accuracy. A typical large egg in the UK (or extra-large in the US) weighs about 55g (2oz) once cracked.

FLOUR

I prefer to use organic strong white bread flour in my dough recipes. It's cultivated using natural fertilizers, free from pesticides, and offers enhanced nutritional benefits. This flour typically contains 11–13% protein, resulting in higher gluten levels. This increased gluten forms an elastic network, binding the starch and trapping carbon dioxide, helping the dough rise. To maintain consistent results in my baking, I stick to the same brand of flour.

FREEZE-DRIED BERRIES

With a fantastic intense flavour, freeze-dried berry powder is a delicious addition to buns, cakes and buttercreams. You can buy it easily online. Large freeze-dried berry pieces are often available at supermarkets and make a lovely, though not essential, topping for buns such as the Danish Lent Buns (see pages 81–2).

MILK
Full-fat milk is the least processed and contains a host of vitamins and omega-3 fats, unlike semi-skimmed and skimmed milk.

NUTS
Nuts add flavour, richness and texture. If you need to store them for more than a month or live in a warm climate, freeze the nuts to prevent the oils from turning rancid and altering their flavour.

SALT
Always use natural fine sea salt in the bun dough, or sea salt flakes (I use Maldon) to top a chocolate or caramel bun.

SPICES
You'll notice I frequently use cardamom in my recipes. I buy green cardamom seeds, already removed from their papery pods, and grind a small amount each time I bake. I highly recommend using freshly ground cardamom. Its fragrance and flavour are far superior to the pre-ground spice.

The cinnamon I use is cassia – also known as bakers' cinnamon. Chinese cassia cinnamon is widely used in Sweden (and the USA) and has a noticeably sweeter flavour profile compared to the verum cinnamon typically used in the UK. Both green cardamom seeds and cassia cinnamon are readily available online.

SUGAR
Sugar gets a bad rep these days, however my recipes don't overdo it; the amount used is meant to enhance flavour, not overpower it. I try to use unrefined sugar, such as golden caster (granulated) or soft light brown sugar.

SUGAR NIBS
Nibbed sugar, also known as pearl sugar, is widely used in different parts of Europe, especially in Scandinavia, Belgium and Italy. These sugar crystals are compressed into nuggets. Thanks to their density, they resist melting during baking, making them ideal for sprinkling on buns. They are readily available online.

YEAST
My first choice is fresh yeast; however, it has become almost impossible to find unless you buy online, which takes the spontaneity out of baking. So, I use fast-action dry yeast in the dough recipes in this book. Once opened, it's stored in the fridge and keeps for several months.

KEY
Recipes marked with **VO** (vegan option) can be made vegan with a few simple swaps. See page 153 for a full list of recipes and more info.

TIPS

When it comes to making sweet enriched buns, the details matter. Whether you're an experienced baker or a newcomer to baking, understanding these foundational tips will help ensure your buns turn out perfectly every time.

USE ROOM-TEMPERATURE INGREDIENTS

Leave all the ingredients out for a while before baking. Milk does not need to be heated to 37°C (99°F) because the temperature of the dough will rise a few degrees during kneading.

WEIGH ALL THE INGREDIENTS IN GRAMS

Baking is like chemistry – accuracy is key to great results. Because of this, I weigh all my ingredients, even liquid ones, although some very small quantities are given in teaspoons.

FREEZING DOUGH

You can freeze unbaked buns with a butter filling, for example Nordic Cinnamon (see page 106), Cardamom (see page 73) and Saffron, Almond and Orange (see page 131), and unfilled buns, such as Semlor (see pages 135–36) or White Chocolate and Passion Fruit (see page pages 144–45). This must be done once they have been shaped, and before proving. Lay them on a lined baking tray and place in the freezer. Once frozen, transfer to freezer bags and place back in the freezer until you're ready to use them. They can stay in the freezer for up to a week.

When you're ready to bake, thaw the buns in the fridge overnight, then prove at room temperature, remembering to space the buns out. Alternatively, you can prove them in the oven (switched off) with a shallow dish of boiling water placed at the bottom. Check them frequently and replace the boiling water a couple of times, as needed.

BAKED BUNS

Can be frozen on the day of baking. However, buns containing custard or cream cheese fillings cannot. To warm through frozen and defrosted buns, heat them in a medium oven (about 140°C fan/325°F, gas 3), for 6–8 minutes.

SPICES

In order to maximize flavours, you need to use freshly ground spices (see page 15).

Baking with yeast involves a few key steps to ensure your buns turn out perfectly. Here's a simplified guide:

PREPARING YOUR INGREDIENTS

Before we go through the process of making enriched yeasted dough, it's crucial to highlight the importance of preparation. Weigh and set out all your ingredients before you start mixing. I have the butter, eggs, milk, sugar and other dry ingredients ready. One advantage of this method is that having all the ingredients at the same temperature helps the dough combine more effectively.

MIXING AND KNEADING

First, combine the ingredients. Once mixed, the dough must be kneaded. Kneading is crucial because it develops the gluten, which gives the bread its structure. Ideally use a stand mixer, although you can do it by hand: combine the ingredients in a large bowl until a dough forms, knead on the work surface for at least 12 minutes, then do the windowpane test (see below).

Why kneading matters: Gluten is a network of proteins that gives bread its elasticity and chewiness and traps air, helping the buns to rise as the trapped air expands with the heat. Proper kneading ensures that these proteins are well developed, which helps the dough rise properly.

The windowpane test: To check if the dough is ready, you can do the windowpane test (see page 27). Take a small piece of dough and stretch it gently between your fingers. If it stretches into a thin, translucent 'window', without tearing, the gluten is fully developed, and you're ready for the next step.

FIRST RISE (BULK FERMENTATION)

After kneading, place the dough in a clean bowl and cover with a dampened dish towel. Let the dough rise; this is called bulk fermentation, and is a crucial step in the bread-making process. It occurs after the dough has been mixed and before it is shaped. During this stage, the dough is left to ferment in bulk (as a single mass) without being divided or shaped.

How long to let it rise: The time needed for this first rise can vary depending on the temperature, but it generally takes about 1–2 hours at average room temperature. You'll know it's ready when it has doubled in size. If you're new to baking and want to try the tangzhong method (see page 34), allow the dough to bulk ferment in the fridge overnight (up to 12 hours). This will make the dough much easier to handle.

KNOCKING BACK AND SHAPING THE DOUGH

Once the dough has risen, deflate it by gently pressing it down with your fist. This is called knocking back. Knocking back dough is an essential step in bread making that helps ensure a well-textured bread. This process involves gently deflating the dough after bulk fermentation to redistribute the yeast, sugars and nutrients; it also promotes even fermentation during the second rise. Knocking back releases excess gas, preventing large air pockets and allowing for a uniform crumb structure. Additionally, it strengthens the gluten network, enhancing the dough's elasticity and structure, which is crucial for shaping. Once knocked back, shape the buns according to the recipe.

SECOND RISE (PROVING)

After shaping, the dough must rise again. This is called proving. At this stage, the dough will rise and double in size. To prove, place the buns on a prepared baking sheet, spaced well apart to allow for expansion.

Proving in the oven: To speed up the proving, you can place the buns (no need to cover them) in the oven, switched off, and place a bowl of freshly boiled water on the floor of the oven. Yeast proves well in a warm and damp environment, so the steam will help the buns rise. When they're ready to bake, remove from the oven and place them on the work surface for 5 minutes so that the condensation from the steamy oven dries from the surface of the buns.

Knowing when the dough is ready to bake: The dough is fully proved when it has expanded and feels slightly springy to the touch. You can test this by gently pressing a finger into the dough; if the indentation slowly springs back, it's ready to bake.

BAKING

Finally, bake the dough in a preheated oven. The exact temperature and time will depend on the recipe. During baking, the dough will expand further (called oven spring) and the crust will form and brown.

Once you get the hang of these steps, baking with yeast is straightforward and so rewarding!

A final note on the basic and tangzhong doughs: Both the basic and tangzhong methods work well for all the recipes in this book. However, I highly recommend using only the tangzhong method for the filled buns, as specified. If you're new to baking, I recommend using the basic dough for all the recipes that require rolling the dough with a rolling pin.

ESSENTIAL EQUIPMENT

These are the must-have tools that are crucial for successful baking:

SHALLOW BAKING TRAYS
Line them with baking paper or use silicone mats.

DIGITAL SCALE
Essential for precise measurements in baking. Weighing ingredients, including liquids, in grams ensures accuracy and consistency in the recipes.

DOUGH SCRAPER
An invaluable tool for handling bread dough. It helps scoop dough out of bowls and clean work surfaces effectively.

ROLLING PIN
Vital for shaping dough, especially when making buns. A wooden or bamboo rolling pin works perfectly.

OVEN
A fan-assisted oven is ideal for even baking, but a conventional oven can also work with adjusted baking times to ensure even results. Increase the oven temperatures provided in these recipes by 20°C if using a conventional oven.

SMALL WHISK
Useful for creating smooth mixtures, like tangzhong dough, by whisking milk and flour without lumps.

PIPING BAG AND PLAIN NOZZLE
Essential for creating smooth mixtures, such as whisking milk and flour together without lumps for tangzhong dough.

NICE-TO-HAVE EQUIPMENT

These tools aren't strictly necessary, but can offer added convenience:

PIZZA ROLLER
Makes dividing dough quick and easy, providing clean cuts. You can use a large, sharp knife as an alternative.

PASTRY TAMPER
Handy for making dough indentations to fill with custard or sweet cheese fillings. A small glass could be used instead.

STAND MIXER
Excellent for making enriched yeasted dough. Although a significant investment, it simplifies mixing and kneading for avid bakers.

BLENDING AND GRINDING TOOLS
A spice grinder is useful for grinding cardamom seeds, and a high-speed blender can purée fruit and make small quantities of nut butters and pastes. A pestle and mortar can also be used for grinding.

MUFFIN TRAYS
Used in several of the recipes in this book, they help give the buns a uniform shape. Muffin trays provide a practical and reliable way to achieve consistent results.

DOU

GHS

Here you'll find a collection of recipes for bun doughs: both basic enriched and the tangzhong method. As well as the standard recipes, this chapter includes vegan options for both doughs.

This book is designed so that you can flick through the Buns chapter (pages 42–147), select a recipe and then select a dough of your choice from the following pages. As I've mentioned before, I'd highly recommend using the tangzhong method for the filled buns and the basic dough for recipes that require rolling.

Once you have decided on your bun and corresponding dough, read through the full recipe for the bun before making a start on your dough, as the dough may require slight tweaks at particular stages.

BASIC ENRICHED DOUGH

This is my go-to dough recipe when time isn't on my side. It's quicker to make this basic enriched dough than the tanzhong method (see pages 34–37), as there's no need to make a separate paste for this recipe. It's vital to knead the dough for at least 12 minutes, as this develops gluten, a network of proteins in the flour. Kneading also strengthens the dough, making it less likely to tear during shaping and rising. This strength is crucial for maintaining the bread's structure as it bakes. I often prove this dough in the fridge, overnight.

MAKES ENOUGH FOR 10 BUNS

345g (12oz) strong white bread flour
5g (1½ tsp) fast-action dried yeast
65g (2¼oz) unsalted butter, softened
40g (1½oz) golden caster (granulated) sugar
½ tsp fine sea salt
55g (2oz) full-fat milk, at room temperature
40g (1½oz) beaten egg, at room temperature
100g (3½oz) water

1

Put the flour, yeast, butter, sugar and salt in a large bowl, along with the milk, egg and water. Mix to combine. Once the dough has come together, knead for 15–18 minutes by hand. Alternatively, add the ingredients to the bowl of a stand mixer with the dough hook attached. Mix on a slow speed until a dough forms. Once the dough has come together, increase the speed to medium–high and work the dough for at least 12 minutes – no less. Don't be tempted to add more flour. To check the dough is ready to prove, do the windowpane test: take a small portion of dough and stretch it out until a thin film forms in the middle without breaking. The dough must be thin enough for light to pass through it. If this doesn't happen, knead for a little longer. When it's ready, you'll have a silky smooth dough that's soft and elastic.

2

Scrape down the sides of the bowl with a dough scraper and tip the dough onto the work surface. With a firm hand, shape the dough into a round with a nice smooth surface on top by using the dough scraper or cupped hands. The dough may stick to the work surface as you rotate it. Lift it, with the aid of the dough scraper, into a lidded container or bowl, large enough for the dough to expand. Either place in the fridge overnight (up to 12 hours) or bulk ferment at room temperature for 1–1½ hours, or until doubled in size (this will depend on your room temperature).

3

The dough is now ready to knock back (see page 18) and shape (see relevant recipe).

VEGAN BASIC ENRICHED DOUGH

In this recipe, I've chosen to use cold-pressed rapeseed (canola) oil that's natural, unrefined and locally produced. It has a golden hue and a delicate, nutty flavour. Many unrefined organic oils are worth noting for their exceptional origin and taste. I've also reduced the quantity of oil compared to my traditional basic dough recipe, as the high quality justifies its cost. I recommend avoiding cheap, highly refined oils.

MAKES ENOUGH FOR 10 BUNS

345g (12oz) strong white bread flour
5g (1½ tsp) fast-action dried yeast
45g (1½oz) cold-pressed rapeseed (canola) oil
20g (¾oz) golden caster (granulated) sugar
½ tsp fine sea salt
75g (2½oz) unsweetened oat or soya milk, at room temperature
20g (¾oz) agave syrup
120g (4¼oz) water

NOTE: Bun recipes that include a vegan option (with a few simple swaps) are marked with a **VO** symbol (see a full list of recipes on page 153)

1

Put the flour, yeast, oil, sugar and salt in a large bowl, along with the milk, agave syrup and water. Mix to combine. Once the dough has come together, knead for 15–18 minutes. Alternatively, add the ingredients to the the bowl of a stand mixer with the dough hook attached. Mix on a slow speed until a dough forms. Once the dough has come together, increase the speed to medium–high and work the dough for at least 12 minutes – no less. Don't be tempted to add more flour. To check the dough is ready to prove, do the windowpane test: take a small portion of dough and stretch it out until a thin film forms in the middle without breaking. The dough must be thin enough for light to pass through it. If this doesn't happen, knead for a little longer. When it's ready, you'll have a silky smooth dough that's soft and elastic.

2

Scrape down the sides of the bowl with a dough scraper and tip the dough onto the work surface. With a firm hand, shape the dough into a round with a nice smooth surface on top by using the dough scraper or cupped hands. The dough may stick to the work surface as you rotate it. Lift it, with the aid of the dough scraper, into a plastic container with a lid, large enough for the dough to expand. Either place in the fridge overnight (up to 12 hours) or bulk ferment at room temperature for 1–1½ hours, or until doubled in size (this will depend on your room temperature).

3

The dough is now ready to knock back (see page 18) and shape (see relevant recipe).

TANGZHONG METHOD DOUGH

Tangzhong is a technique used in bread making – particularly popular in East Asian baking – to create soft and fluffy bread with a longer shelf life. It involves cooking a portion of the flour and liquid into a thick paste before adding it to the rest of the ingredients. It is a little more difficult to handle than the basic recipe, therefore I recommend bulk fermenting this dough in the fridge, overnight. The dough will then be easier to handle.

MAKES ENOUGH FOR 10 BUNS

TANGZHONG
16g (½oz) strong white bread flour
80g (2¾oz) full-fat milk

ENRICHED DOUGH
330g (11½oz) strong white bread flour
5g (1½ tsp) fast-action dried yeast
65g (2¼oz) unsalted butter, softened
40g (1½oz) golden caster (granulated) sugar
¼ tsp fine sea salt
145g (5oz) full-fat milk, at room temperature
40g (1½oz) beaten egg, at room temperature

1

To make the tangzhong, put the milk and flour in a small saucepan and whisk together until smooth. Set the pan over a medium heat and briskly mix with a small balloon whisk until it thickens and bubbles. Continue to cook for a few seconds or so until thickened, then remove from the heat and use a rubber spatula to scrape all the tangzhong into a bowl. Cover the surface of the mixture with a disc of baking paper. Once cooled to room temperature, it's ready to use.

2

To make the dough, put the flour, yeast, butter, sugar and salt in a large bowl, along with the milk and egg. Mix to combine. Once the dough has come together, add the tangzhong and knead for 15–18 minutes. Alternatively, add the dough ingredients to the bowl of a stand mixer with the dough hook attached. Mix on a slow speed until a dough forms. Once the dough has come together, add the tangzhong, increase the speed to medium–high and work the dough for at least 12 minutes – no less. Don't be tempted to add more flour. To check the dough is ready to prove, do the windowpane test: take a small portion of dough and stretch it out until a thin film forms in the middle without breaking. The dough must be thin enough for light to pass through it. If this doesn't happen, knead for a little longer. When it's ready, you'll have a silky smooth dough that's bouncy and elastic.

3

Scrape down the sides of the bowl with a dough scraper and tip the dough onto the work surface. With a firm hand, shape the dough into a round with a nice smooth surface on the top by using the dough scraper or cupped hands. The dough may stick to the work surface as you rotate it. Lift it, with the aid of the dough scraper, into a plastic container with a lid, large enough for the dough to expand. Either place in the fridge overnight to bulk ferment (up to 12 hours) or in a warm place for 1–1½ hours, or until doubled in size. (This will depend on the room temperature.)

4

The dough is now ready to knock back (see page 18) and shape (see relevant recipe).

VEGAN TANGZHONG METHOD DOUGH

I recommend bulk fermenting this dough in the fridge for up to 12 hours. It will be easier to handle, if you're new to baking.

MAKES ENOUGH FOR 10 BUNS

TANGZHONG
16g (½oz) strong white bread flour
80g (2¾oz) unsweetened oat or soya milk

ENRICHED DOUGH
330g (11½oz) strong white bread flour
5g (1½ tsp) fast-action dried yeast
45g (1½oz) cold-pressed rapeseed (canola) oil
20g (¾oz) golden caster (granulated) sugar
20g (¾oz) agave syrup
½ tsp fine sea salt
180g (6¼oz) unsweetened oat or soya milk, at room temperature

NOTE: Bun recipes that include a vegan option (with a few simple swaps) are marked with a **VO** symbol (see a full list of recipes on page 153)

1

To make the tangzhong, put the flour and milk in a small saucepan and whisk together until smooth. Set the pan over a medium heat and briskly mix with a small balloon whisk until it thickens and bubbles. Continue to cook for a few seconds or so until thickened, then remove from the heat and use a rubber spatula to scrape all the tangzhong into a bowl. Cover the surface of the mixture with a disc of baking paper. Once cooled to room temperature, it's ready to use.

2

To make the dough, put the flour, yeast, oil, sugar, agave and salt in a large bowl, along with the milk. Mix to combine. Once the dough has come together, add the tangzhong and knead for 15–18 minutes. Alternatively, add the dough ingredients to the bowl of a stand mixer with the dough hook attached. Mix on a slow speed until a dough forms. Once the dough has come together, add the tangzhong, increase the speed to medium–high and work the dough for at least 12 minutes – no less. Don't be tempted to add more flour, it will all come together.

To check the dough is ready to prove, do the windowpane test: take a small portion of dough and stretch it out until a thin film forms in the middle without breaking. The dough must be thin enough for light to pass through it. If this doesn't happen, knead for a little longer. When it's ready, you'll have a silky smooth dough that's bouncy and elastic.

3

Scrape down the sides of the bowl with a dough scraper and tip the dough onto the work surface. With a firm hand, shape the dough into a round with a nice smooth surface on the top by using the dough scraper or cupped hands. The dough may stick to the work surface as you rotate it. Lift it, with the aid of the dough scraper, into a plastic container with a lid, large enough for the dough to expand. Either place in the fridge overnight to bulk ferment (up to 12 hours) or in a warm place for 1–1½ hours or until doubled in size. (This will depend on the room temperature.)

4

The dough is now ready to knock back (see page 18) and shape (see relevant recipe).

B

UNS

Here you'll find a collection of recipes for buns with influences from many different countries. There are classics and traditional favourites, as well as playful flavour combinations that work nicely together. Some make the most of fresh, seasonal produce, while others celebrate store-cupboard heroes and even stale buns (see Spiced Pear and Pecan Buns, page 138). You'll find a delicious variety of tastes and textures in these pages. For each bun, I've recommended a particular dough method.

AMERICAN-STYLE CINNAMON ROLLS

This is my version of the all-American classic. I've reduced the sugar and added a little more naturally sweet cinnamon. Soft, fluffy and full of warm spice, these rolls strike the perfect balance between indulgence and comfort.

MAKES 9 BUNS

1 recipe quantity Basic Enriched Dough (see page 26)
strong white bread flour, for dusting

FILLING
70g (2½oz) unsalted butter
60g (2¼oz) soft light brown sugar
1½ tbsp ground cinnamon

CREAM CHEESE FROSTING
40g (1½oz) unsalted butter, softened
75g (2½oz) icing (confectioners') sugar
1½ tsp Vanilla Sugar (see page 150)
90g (3¼oz) full-fat cream cheese, at room temperature
a good pinch of salt

Line a 25 x 20cm (10 x 8 inch) baking dish with baking paper.

Knock back the dough, then on a lightly floured work surface, roll out the dough to a rectangle measuring approximately 45 x 26cm (17¾ x 10½ inches), lifting it a few times during rolling to release the tension in the dough. Spread the butter for the filling evenly over the dough with an offset spatula.

In a bowl, combine the sugar and cinnamon. Sprinkle this mixture evenly over the buttered dough. Working carefully, from a long edge, roll the dough away from you into a tight roll and seal the end with a little water. Cut the rolled dough into 9 thick slices (I use heavy-duty cotton thread for this).

Place the cinnamon rolls, cut-sides up, in the baking dish, leaving some space between each one. Now cover the rolls with a lightly dampened dish towel and leave them to prove until they have doubled in size, about 1–1½ hours.

Towards the end of the proving time, preheat the oven to 180°C fan (400°C), gas 6.

Bake the rolls in the preheated oven for approximately 20–25 minutes, or until they turn golden brown.

While the rolls are baking, prepare the cream cheese frosting. In a bowl, cream together the butter, icing sugar and vanilla sugar until light and fluffy. Now add the cream cheese and salt, and whisk until smooth.

Once the rolls are baked, remove them from the oven and transfer, with the baking paper, to a wire rack. Leave to cool for approximately 25 minutes. While the rolls are still a little warm, spread the cream cheese frosting over the top, allowing it to melt into the rolls.

Store in an airtight container. Best eaten on the day or the day after baking.

APPLE & CINNAMON

I love the soothing combination of apple and cinnamon. While I'm not fond of Granny Smith apples for eating raw, they have a lovely tart–sweet flavour once cooked. The warm, spicy notes of cinnamon enhance the sweetness of the purée. Whichever dessert apple you choose, make sure it's a tart one.

MAKES 10 BUNS | **VO** (see page 153)

1 recipe quantity Basic Enriched Dough (see page 26)
strong white bread flour, for dusting
30g (1oz) sugar nibs
Sugar Syrup (see page 148), for brushing

APPLE PURÉE
2–3 Granny Smith apples (or your favourite tart apple, about 450g/1lb total weight)
60g (2¼oz) soft light brown sugar
2 tsp lemon juice
1 tbsp water
10g (⅓oz) unsalted butter

FILLING
95g (3¼oz) unsalted butter, softened
45g (2½oz) golden caster (granulated) sugar
2 tbsp ground cinnamon

EGG WASH
1 large egg
1 tsp water
a pinch of fine sea salt

Peel and core the apples, then cut them into small dice. Place in a saucepan with the sugar, lemon juice and water. Bring to a simmer, then cover with a lid. Cook for 8–10 minutes, removing the lid in the last few minutes so the purée can thicken. The apples should be soft and cooked through. Mash with a potato masher, leaving some texture. Now stir the butter through the purée. Set aside to cool.

For the filling, mix the butter with the sugar and cinnamon to form a smooth paste. Set aside.

Line two baking trays with baking paper.

Knock back the dough. On a lightly floured work surface, roll out the dough to a rectangle measuring 74 x 24cm (29 x 9½ inches), lifting it a few times during rolling to release the tension in the dough. Spread the cinnamon butter evenly over the entire surface of the dough with an offset spatula. Now fold the dough in half, taking the top to the bottom – it should measure 37 x 24cm (14½ x 9½ inches). With a pizza roller, cut into 10 even strips.

Place the end of a dough strip flat on the work surface, then coil the dough round loosely to form a rosette, tucking the end under. You should not have any gaps at the bottom of the bun; you don't want any filling to escape. Repeat to make 10 buns.

Place the buns on the lined baking trays, making sure they have space to expand. Now create a cavity in each cavity. Place a heaped teaspoon of apple purée in the centre of each bun, pushing it down into the buns as much as possible.

Cover the buns and leave to prove for 1–1½ hours, or until the dough springs back when you press your finger gently into it.

Towards the end of the proving time, preheat the oven to 190°C fan (410°C), gas 6, and whisk together all the ingredients for the egg wash.

Brush the buns with egg wash and sprinkle with sugar nibs. Bake for 10–12 minutes, or until golden.

When the buns are ready, brush with a little sugar syrup and leave to cool on a wire rack. Best eaten on the day of baking.

APRICOT & LAVENDER

Finding really good fresh apricots can be quite challenging, as they are often dry and tasteless. However, once cooked, they transform into something truly special. This is why I usually opt to bake them or make preserves. Frangipane pairs perfectly with apricots, and a touch of lavender adds a lovely floral note. Plums would be a nice alternative to apricots. Pictured on page 53.

MAKES 10 BUNS

strong white bread flour, for dusting
1 recipe quantity Basic Enriched Dough (see page 26)
4 apricots, cut into thirds

FRANGIPANE
1 tbsp plain (all-purpose) flour
80g (2¾oz) ground almonds
100g (3½oz) unsalted butter, softened
100g (3½oz) caster (granulated) sugar
1 large egg, beaten
petals stripped from 3 lavender heads (or 1 tsp dried culinary lavender)

EGG WASH
1 large egg
1 tsp water
a pinch of fine sea salt

VANILLA FILLING
60g (2oz) unsalted butter
30g (1oz) golden caster (granulated) sugar
1 tsp Vanilla Sugar (see page 150)

LAVENDER-INFUSED SYRUP
3 tbsp light brown sugar
3 tbsp water
petals stripped from 3–4 lavender heads (or 2 tsp dried culinary lavender), plus optional extra to decorate

Recipe continues overleaf

Begin with the frangipane: combine the flour and ground almonds and set aside.

Beat the butter and sugar together until light and fluffy. Gradually add the egg, beating between each addition. Now fold in the almond mixture and lavender petals. Set aside.

Whisk together the ingredients for the egg wash and set aside.

Next make the vanilla filling: with a rubber spatula, blend the butter, sugar and vanilla sugar. Set aside.

Line two large baking sheets with baking paper.

Knock back the dough. On a lightly floured work surface, roll out the dough to a rectangle measuring approximately 74 x 23cm (29 x 9 inches), lifting it a few times during rolling to release the tension in the dough. Spread the filling evenly over the dough with an offset spatula. With a short edge of the rectangle in front of you, fold the dough in half, bringing the top edge down to the bottom, making sure the edges meet; it should measure 37 x 23cm (14½ x 9 inches).

With a pizza roller or large knife, cut the dough into 10 strips along the short edge, each approximately 23mm (1 inch) wide. Place the end of a dough strip flat on the work surface, then coil the dough round loosely to form a rosette, tucking the end under. You should not have any gaps at the bottom of the bun; you don't want any filling to escape. Now make an indentation in the centre to create a cavity. Place a small spoonful of frangipane in the cavity, pushing it down into the bun as much as possible (you will have a little more than you need for this recipe). Now top with a third of an apricot. Repeat to coil all the dough strips and assemble 10 buns. Place the buns on the lined baking sheets, cover with a lightly dampened dish towel and leave to prove for 1–1½ hours, or until the dough springs back when you press your finger gently into it.

Towards the end of the proving time, preheat the oven to 185°C fan (405°F), gas 6.

Once proved, brush the buns with the egg wash and bake for 12–14 minutes, or until golden.

While the buns are baking, make the lavender-infused syrup. Put the sugar, water and lavender petals in a small saucepan. Gently bring to a simmer and cook until syrupy. Remove from the heat.

When the buns are ready, brush them with the lavender syrup. Sprinkle over a few lavender petals to decorate, if desired.

Best eaten on the day, or the day after baking. Store in an airtight container, or freeze on the day of baking for up to 3 months; once defrosted, warm in a medium oven for 5–8 minutes.

BLACKBERRY OAT CRUMBLE

When the hedgerows are teeming with blackberries, I find it hard to resist filling my basket with this late summer fruit. A variation on the Polish *drożdżówki*, I've tried to replicate the sour cheese flavour in these buns by incorporating sour cream into the filling. Pictured on pages 56–7.

MAKES 10 BUNS

1 recipe quantity Tangzhong Method Dough (see page 34)
strong white bread flour, for dusting
icing (confectioners') sugar, to dust (optional)

BLACKBERRY COMPOTE
200g (7oz) blackberries
45g (2½oz) golden caster (granulated) sugar
1 bay leaf
1 tsp lemon juice
1 tsp cornflour (cornstarch)
1 tsp cold water

OAT CRUMBLE
60g (2¼oz) plain (all-purpose) flour
15g (½oz) porridge oats
30g (1oz) demerara (light brown or turbinado) sugar
a pinch of salt
50g (1¾oz) unsalted butter, cold

Begin with the blackberry compote: wash the berries and place them in a small saucepan with the sugar, bay leaf and lemon juice. Bring to a simmer and cook for 5–8 minutes, or until they break down and the juice is released from the berries. Remove from the heat and leave for 5 minutes to cool a little. Mix the cornflour with the cold water, then add to the compote and stir. Return to a medium heat and simmer for 3–4 minutes, or until thickened. Pour into a bowl and leave to cool completely.

For the crumble, put the flour, oats, sugar and salt in a small bowl. Cut the butter into small dice and rub it in with your fingertips until the mixture resembles moist breadcrumbs. Shake the bowl and any big bits will come to the surface – rub them in.

Line two baking trays with baking paper.

Knock back the dough, then weigh and divide it into 10 even pieces. To shape the buns, add a very small amount of flour to the work surface, then place your cupped hand over a portion of the dough. Roll the dough in a circular motion until it's perfectly round, then place on the prepared tray. Repeat to shape all the buns. Cover with a lightly dampened dish towel and leave them to prove for about 1–1½ hours, or until doubled in size.

Towards the end of the proving time, preheat the oven to 190°C fan (410°C), gas 6.

SWEET CHEESE FILLING
160g (5¾oz) full-fat cream cheese, at room temperature
40g (1½oz) sour cream
45g (1½oz) golden caster (granulated) sugar
1½ tsp Vanilla Sugar (see page 150)
1 egg yolk

EGG WASH
1 large egg
1 tsp water
a pinch of fine sea salt

Combine all the sweet cheese filling ingredients in a bowl. Set aside. Whisk together all the ingredients for the egg wash and set this aside, too.

Have ready a small pastry tamper or glass measuring 4cm (1½ inches) in diameter at the base. Sprinkle a little flour on the centre of a bun so that the tamper doesn't stick. Dip the tamper in flour, shaking off the excess, and use it to make an indentation in the centre of the bun. Repeat to make an indentation in all the buns. Now brush the surface of the buns with the egg wash. Place a spoonful of the sweet cheese filling in the centre of each, pushing the spoon down so the filling is sitting in the dough nicely. Follow with a spoonful of the compote. Finally, sprinkle with the oat crumble.

Bake the buns for 12–14 minutes, or until golden. They are delicious eaten warm, dusted with a little icing sugar. Best eaten on the day of baking.

BLUEBERRY & CREAM CHEESE

Sweet, creamy and tangy. What better way to celebrate the little indigo berries of summer than in a fluffy blueberry cream cheese bun? I've used freeze-dried blueberry powder in this recipe, which you can find easily online. It has a fantastic intense flavour. It's delicious in smoothies or stirred into Greek yogurt for breakfast, too.

MAKES 10 BUNS

1 recipe quantity Basic Enriched Dough (see page 26)
strong white bread flour, for dusting
30g (1oz) sugar nibs
Sugar Syrup (see page 148), for brushing

FILLING
1½ tbsp freeze-dried blueberry powder
75g (2½oz) full-fat cream cheese, at room temperature
15g (½oz) unsalted butter, softened
55g (2oz) icing (confectioners') sugar
finely grated zest of ½ lemon

EGG WASH
1 large egg
1 tsp water
a pinch of fine sea salt

TIP: These are also delicious with 1½ tablespoons of freshly ground cardamom added to the dough.

Begin by preparing the filling: sift the freeze-dried blueberry powder into a bowl to get rid of any clumps. Now add the remaining filling ingredients and whisk together until smooth. Set aside.

Line two baking trays with baking paper.

Knock back the dough. On a lightly floured work surface, roll out the dough to a rectangle measuring approximately 54 x 30cm (20¾ x 12 inches), lifting it a few times during rolling to release the tension in the dough. Spread the blueberry filling evenly over the dough with an offset spatula. With a short edge towards you, fold the dough in three, folding the bottom third up to cover the middle and the top third down to cover that. Gently roll out the dough again to a rectangle measuring 17 x 35cm (6½ x 14 inches).

With a pizza roller or large knife, cut the dough into 10 wide strips, each measuring approximately 35mm (1½ inches) across. Cut along the length of a strip through the middle, almost to the top (it should look like a pair of trousers). Now twist the two strands of dough in different directions, twisting one clockwise and the other anti-clockwise, then tie them in a knot. Repeat to shape all the buns. Some of the filling will escape, so rinse your hands between each shaping. Once shaped, place the buns on the lined baking sheets. Cover with a lightly dampened dish towel and leave them to prove for about 1–1½ hours, or until doubled in size.

Towards the end of the proving time, preheat the oven to 190°C fan (410°C), gas 6, and whisk together all the ingredients for the egg wash.

Brush the buns with the egg wash and shower them with sugar nibs. Bake for 10–12 minutes, or until golden brown. As soon as they come out of the oven, brush with a little sugar syrup. Leave to cool on a wire rack. Best eaten on the day of baking.

BLUEBERRY SUGAR

Blueberries evoke memories of summers spent in Sweden. We'd take our baskets into the forest, not far from my uncle's summer house, to pick (and devour) these deep-purple berries. With stained fingers, we'd gather at the house to sort through our bounty, using them to bake cakes, make cordials, or freeze to enjoy during the winter months. The wild berries were a fraction of the size of the commercially grown ones we buy today. I've used freeze-dried blueberry powder here (widely available online) because the flavour is so tart, intense and delicious. A piping bag is useful for this recipe. Pictured on pages 62–3.

MAKES 10 BUNS

25g (1oz) unsalted butter, melted and cooled, plus extra for greasing
1 recipe quantity Tangzhong Method Dough (see page 34)
strong white bread flour, for dusting
1½ tbsp freeze-dried blueberry powder
45g (1½oz) caster (granulated) sugar
edible flowers, to decorate (optional)

VANILLA CREAM
200g (7oz) full-fat milk
3 egg yolks (55–60g/2–2¼oz)
40g (1½oz) caster (granulated) sugar
2 tsp Vanilla Sugar (see page 150) or 1 tsp vanilla bean paste
2 tbsp cornflour (cornstarch)
12g (½oz) unsalted butter, chilled and cut into small dice
55g (2oz) double (heavy) cream

Begin with the vanilla cream: ideally, make this the day before you plan to make the buns. Bring the milk to the boil in a small saucepan. In a separate bowl, beat the egg yolks, sugar, vanilla sugar and cornflour until pale and fluffy. In a steady stream, pour the hot milk onto the egg mixture, beating continuously. Pour the mixture back into the saucepan and heat, beating all the time, until it thickens and boils. Pour into a cold bowl. Add the diced butter to the custard, beating until it is completely incorporated. Cover the surface with a disc of baking paper. Transfer to the fridge when cool.

Once the custard is cold, take a handheld electric whisk and beat it until it's smooth. Whip the double cream to soft peaks, then fold it into the vanilla cream. Place in the fridge until needed.

Grease a muffin tin with melted butter.

Knock back the dough, weigh and divide it into 10 equal pieces. To shape the buns, add a very small amount of flour to the work surface, then place your cupped hand over a portion of the dough. Move your cupped hand in a quick, tight circular motion – this will cause the seam to come together, create tension on the surface of the dough and make the bun perfectly round. Repeat to shape all the buns, then place the buns in the greased muffin tin. Cover with a lightly dampened dish towel and leave to prove for 1–1½ hours, depending on the room temperature, until doubled in size.

Towards the end of the proving time, preheat the oven to 190°C fan (410°C), gas 6.

Bake the buns for 12–14 minutes, or until golden and sounding hollow when the undersides are tapped. Leave to cool on a wire rack.

Pass the blueberry powder through a fine sieve into a shallow bowl to remove any lumps. Add the sugar and mix well.

Spoon the vanilla cream into a piping bag fitted with a 1cm (½ inch) plain nozzle.

With a small, serrated knife, cut a hole in the top of the bun (about 1cm/½ inch in diameter) and hollow out a small amount of the crumb. Now brush the top halves with the melted butter, then dip and roll the top of each bun in blueberry sugar to coat.

Use your piping bag to fill the buns with the vanilla cream, finishing with a small swirl on the top and a few edible flower petals, if wished. Store the buns at room temperature, as they become dry in the fridge. They can be filled a few hours before serving.

TIP: These are also delicious made with freeze-dried raspberry or strawberry powder.

BROWN BUTTER & VANILLA

Brown butter is incredibly delicious because it undergoes a heat process that causes the milk solids to caramelize and develop a rich, nutty flavour. This transformation adds depth and complexity to the butter. That said, the flavour is delicate, so don't overdo the vanilla.

MAKES 10 BUNS

1 recipe quantity Basic Enriched Dough (see page 26)
strong white bread flour, for dusting
Vanilla Sugar (see page 150), for dusting

BROWN BUTTER FILLING
120g (4¼oz) unsalted butter, diced, plus extra for greasing
15g (½oz) Vanilla Sugar (see page 150)
30g (1oz) golden caster (granulated) sugar

EGG WASH
1 large egg
1 tsp water
a pinch of fine sea salt

Begin with the brown butter filling. Place the diced butter in a small saucepan over a medium heat. Cook the butter, swirling the pan occasionally, until it becomes foamy. Once you reach this point, keep an eye on it as it will turn quite quickly. Keep swirling the pan so you can see what is going on under the foam. You're looking for the butter to be amber and the milk deposits brown. Remove from heat and pour into a bowl. Be sure to scrape out all the little flecks of brown in the bottom of the pan – they are toasted milk solids and are full of flavour. Leave to set. Once firm, mix with the vanilla and caster sugars.

Grease a muffin tray with butter.

Knock back the dough. On a lightly floured work surface, roll out the prepared dough to a rectangle measuring approximately 54 x 30cm (21¼ x 12 inches), lifting it a few times during rolling to release the tension in the dough. Spread the brown butter filling all over the surface of the dough with an offset spatula. With a short edge towards you, fold the dough in three, folding the bottom third up to cover the middle and the top third down to cover that. Gently roll out the dough again to a rectangle measuring 21 x 35cm (8¼ x 14 inches).

Recipe continues overleaf

With a pizza roller or large knife, cut the dough into 10 wide strips, each measuring approximately 35mm (1½ inches) across. Cut along the length of a strip through the middle, almost to the top (it should look like a pair of trousers). Now twist the two strands of dough in different directions, twisting one clockwise and the other anti-clockwise, then tie them in a knot. Repeat to shape all the buns. Some of the filling will escape, so rinse your hands between each shaping. Once shaped, place the buns in the prepared muffin tray. Cover with a lightly dampened dish towel and leave to prove for about 1–1½ hours, or until doubled in size.

Towards the end of the proving time, preheat the oven to 190°C fan (410°C), gas 6, and whisk together all the ingredients for the egg wash.

Brush the buns with egg wash, trying to avoid brushing too close to the tin or they may stick. Bake for 10–12 minutes, or until golden brown. Remove from the tin and leave to cool on a wire rack.

Once cool, dust lightly with vanilla sugar. Best eaten on the day of baking.

BUN WREATH

A tear-and-share bun wreath never fails to impress. You can choose any flavoured butter or nut-based filling from the book and be sure to shower the wreath with sugar nibs or nuts. It's worth noting it needs a little longer in the oven, but it's so worth the wait.

MAKES 1 WREATH | **VO** (see page 153)

1 recipe quantity of Basic Enriched Dough (see page 26)
strong white bread flour, for dusting
any butter or nut-based filling
sugar nibs, for sprinkling
Sugar Syrup (see page 148)

EGG WASH
1 large egg
1 tsp water
a pinch of fine sea salt

Line a large baking sheet with baking paper.

Knock back the dough. On a lightly floured work surface, roll out the prepared dough to a rectangle measuring approximately 35 x 45cm (14 x 17 inches), lifting it a few times during rolling to release the tension in the dough. Spread your chosen filling evenly over the dough with an offset spatula. With a long edge of the rectangle in front of you, roll the dough up into a long sausage. Fasten the ends together to form a ring – I do this by pushing one end of the sausage into the middle of the other, then pulling the outermost dough over and pressing together (see page 70).

Place the wreath onto the prepared baking sheet, making sure it is arranged in a neat circle in the centre.

With a blunt knife, mark out 12 even segments. Take a pair of sharp kitchen scissors and snip along the marked lines, almost all the way through. Reposition the segments so that they are offset, pushing the first segment one way, then the next in the other direction (see page 71). Cover with a lightly dampened dish towel and leave to prove for 1–1½ hours.

Towards the end of the proving time, preheat the oven to 180°C fan (400°C), gas 6, and whisk together the ingredients for the egg wash.

Brush the entire wreath with the egg wash, then sprinkle with sugar nibs. Bake for about 20–25 minutes until the wreath is golden brown. Remove from the oven and brush immediately with the sugar syrup. Serve warm from the oven. Best eaten on the day of baking.

CARDAMOM BUNS

If I had to choose one spice that epitomizes Scandinavian baking, it would definitely be cardamom. This warm, aromatic spice is a staple in many traditional Scandinavian recipes, adding a distinctive flavour that is both spicy and sweet. These *kardemummabullar* contain a substantial amount of cardamom, making them irresistibly fragrant. Be sure to use freshly ground (see page 15); it makes all the difference.

MAKES 10 BUNS | **VO** (see page 153)

1 recipe quantity Basic Enriched Dough (see page 26), with 1 tbsp freshly ground cardamom added to the flour at step 2
strong white bread flour, for dusting
Sugar Syrup (see page 148)

FILLING
95g (3¼oz) unsalted butter, softened
45g (1¾oz) golden caster (granulated) sugar
1 tbsp freshly ground cardamom

EGG WASH
1 large egg
1 tsp water
a pinch of fine sea salt

TOPPING
2 tbsp golden granulated sugar
2 tsp freshly ground cardamom

Begin with the filling: in a small bowl, blend the butter, sugar and cardamom together using a rubber spatula. Set aside

Line two baking trays with baking paper.

On a lightly floured work surface, roll out the dough to a rectangle measuring 75 x 20cm (30 x 8 inches), lifting it a few times during rolling to release the tension in the dough. Spread the cardamom butter all over the surface of the dough with an offset spatula. Fold the dough in half, making sure the seams meet, then gently roll out again to make a rectangle measuring approximately 40 x 23cm (16 x 9 inches).

With a pizza roller or large knife, cut the dough into 10 strips, each approximately 23mm (1 inch) wide. Twist each strip several times into a spiral around your two fingers, then tuck the end in the gap between your two fingers. This will prevent it unraveling when it bakes. Repeat to shape the rest of the buns.

Place the buns on the lined baking trays, making sure there's space between them for the buns to expand. Cover with a lightly dampened dish towel and leave to prove for 1–1½ hours, or until the dough springs back when you press your finger gently into it.

Towards the end of the proving time, preheat the oven to 190°C fan (410°C), gas 6, and whisk together the ingredients for the egg wash.

Brush the buns with the egg wash. Bake for 10–12 minutes, or until golden.

While the buns are baking, blend the granulated sugar with the ground cardamom. When the buns are ready, brush with a little sugar syrup and sprinkle with the cardamom sugar.

Best eaten on the day of baking; however, they freeze well. After defrosting, just warm through in a medium oven for 5–8 minutes.

CLASSIC CHELSEA BUNS

Chelsea buns are delicious little sticky buns, filled with an abundance of fruit and a subtle warmth from mixed spices. They're simple to make at home and are incredibly satisfying. The buttery dough and sweet honey glaze make them a perfect treat for any occasion, bringing a touch of nostalgia to your table. Pictured on pages 76–7.

MAKES 9 BUNS | **VO** (see page 153)

1 recipe quantity Tangzhong Method Dough (see page 34), with 1 tsp mixed spice blend (see below) added to the flour at step 2
strong white bread flour, for dusting

MIXED SPICE BLEND
1 tbsp ground cinnamon
1 tsp ground coriander
½ tsp ground nutmeg
1½ tsp ground ginger
½ tsp ground allspice
½ tsp ground cloves

FILLING
45g (1½oz) currants
45g (1½oz) raisins
1½ tsp mixed spice blend (see above)
45g (1½oz) unsalted butter, softened
zest of 1 small lemon
45g (1½oz) soft light brown sugar

GLAZE
2 tbsp honey
1 tbsp lemon juice
1 tbsp water

Begin with the mixed spice blend, as you'll need to add this to the dough: combine all the spices in a small jar and set to one side. You won't need all of it for this recipe.

For the filling, soak the dried fruit in boiling water for 30 minutes. Drain and dry with kitchen paper. Blend the mixed spice with the butter and lemon zest and set aside.

Line a 25 x 20cm (10 x 8 inch) baking tin with baking paper.

Knock back the dough. On a lightly floured work surface, roll out the prepared dough to a rectangle measuring approximately 45 x 24cm ($17\frac{3}{4}$ x $9\frac{1}{2}$ inches), lifting it a few times during rolling to release the tension in the dough. Spread the spiced butter mixture evenly over the dough with an offset spatula, leaving a 2cm ($\frac{3}{4}$ inch) gap at the top to seal. Sprinkle over the sugar and mixed fruit.

Working carefully, from a long edge, roll the dough away from you into a tight roll and seal the end with a little water. Cut the rolled dough into 9 thick slices (I use heavy-duty cotton thread for this).

Place the rolls, cut-sides up, in a lined baking dish, leaving a little space between each roll for them to expand. Cover the rolls with a lightly dampened dish towel and leave to prove at room temperature until puffy and the buns are touching each other. This can take 1–$1\frac{1}{2}$ hours, depending on the room temperature.

Towards the end of the proving time, preheat the oven to 175°C fan (385°C), gas 5.

Place the tray in the oven and bake for 20–25 minutes until golden brown. Check after 15 minutes or so and cover the buns with foil if they are getting too brown.

While the rolls are baking, prepare the glaze by stirring together all the ingredients in a small saucepan. Heat gently until syrupy, then leave to cool.

When the rolls are ready, brush them with the glaze. Best eaten on the day of baking.

CHOCOLATE & TAHINI

I am a full-blown tahini obsessive. It's fantastic in cakes, cookies and, of course, savoury dishes. Paired with dark chocolate, it creates my favourite baking combination: slightly bitter, rich and nutty. I've added a little Maldon salt to balance the complex flavours.

MAKES 10 BUNS | **VO** (see page 153)

1 recipe quantity Basic Enriched Dough (see page 26)
strong white bread flour, for dusting
Sugar Syrup (see page 148), for brushing
2 tbsp sesame seeds
sea salt flakes, to sprinkle

FILLING
70g (2½oz) dark chocolate (54% cocoa solids)
70g (2½oz) unsalted butter, cubed
35g (1¼oz) tahini, stirred
3 tbsp icing (confectioners') sugar

EGG WASH
1 large egg
1 tsp water
a pinch of fine sea salt

TIP: These are also delicious with 1½ tablespoons of freshly ground cardamom added to the dough.

Begin with the filling: melt the butter and chocolate together until smooth. You need the mixture to be a spreadable consistency, so pop it in the fridge, but keep an eye on it as you don't want it to thicken too much. Combine the tahini and icing sugar in a separate bowl and set aside.

Line two baking sheets with baking paper.

Knock back the dough. On a lightly floured work surface, roll out the prepared dough to a rectangle measuring approximately 54 x 30cm (21¼ x 12 inches), lifting it a few times during rolling to release the tension in the dough. Spread the chocolate mixture all over the surface of the dough with an offset spatula. Now randomly add teaspoonfuls of the tahini mixture on top of the chocolate. With a short edge towards you, fold the dough in three, folding the bottom third up to cover the middle and the top third down to cover that. Gently roll out the dough again to a rectangle measuring 17 x 35cm (6½ x 14 inches).

With a pizza roller or large knife, cut the dough into 10 wide strips, each measuring approximately 35mm (1½ inches) across. Cut along the length of a strip through the middle, almost to the top (it should look like a pair of trousers). Now twist the two strands of dough in different directions, twisting one clockwise and the other anti-clockwise, then tie them in a knot. Repeat to shape all the buns. Some of the filling may escape, so rinse your hands between each shaping. Place the buns on the lined baking sheets. Cover with a lightly dampened dish towel and leave to prove for 1–1½ hours, or until approximately doubled in size.

Towards the end of the proving time, preheat the oven to 190°C fan (410°C), gas 6, and whisk together all the ingredients for the egg wash.

Brush the buns with the egg wash. Bake for 10–12 minutes, or until golden brown.

As soon as they come out of the oven, brush with a little sugar syrup and sprinkle with the sesame seeds and sea salt flakes. Leave to cool on a wire rack. Best eaten on the day of baking, however, they freeze incredibly well. Once defrosted, just warm in a medium oven for 5–8 minutes.

DANISH LENT BUNS

The Danish version of the Lent bun – *fastelavnsboller*. There's something for everyone in this recipe: it's creamy and sweet, with some acidity, then dark and a little bitter at the same time. The texture of the bun is so fluffy.

1 recipe quantity Tangzhong Method Dough (see page 34) with 1½ tbsp freshly ground cardamom added to the flour in stage 2
strong white bread flour, for dusting
freeze-dried raspberry pieces, to sprinkle

RASPBERRY CREAM
200g (7oz) frozen raspberries
50g (1¾oz) golden caster (granulated) sugar, plus 1 tsp
110g (3¾oz) double (heavy) cream
3 large egg yolks (about 55g/2oz)
15g (½oz) cornflour (cornstarch)
20g (¾oz) unsalted butter, chilled and cut into small dice

EGG WASH
1 large egg
1 tsp water
a pinch of fine sea salt

CHOCOLATE TOPPING
35g (1¼oz) unsalted butter
50g (1¾oz) water
100g (3½oz) dark chocolate chips or good-quality (54% cocoa solids) dark chocolate, finely chopped

Begin by making the raspberry cream: put the raspberries and the teaspoon of sugar in a small saucepan and cook over a medium heat until the fruit is completely broken down and has released all of its juices. Boil for a few minutes until the liquid has thickened. Pass the mixture through a fine sieve into a bowl, pressing down against the seeds with a ladle to make sure you extract as much raspberry liquid as possible. Scrape all of the purée from the underside of the sieve into the bowl with a spatula, then set aside to cool slightly. You should have 120g (4¼oz) of purée.

In a medium saucepan, heat the cream gently. In a separate bowl, combine the egg yolks, 50g sugar and cornflour and whisk until the mixture looks creamy and completely combined.

When the cream has reached a simmer, remove from the heat and whisk it into the egg mixture, then return the mixture to the saucepan. Heat over a medium heat, whisking to stop it cooking unevenly, until the pastry cream has thickened and is just starting to bubble – this should take less than a minute and it will be very thick. Turn off the heat and immediately whisk in the raspberry purée, then add the cold butter, whisking until fully incorporated. Cover the surface directly with a disc of baking paper, to prevent a skin forming. Leave to cool, then place in the fridge for 4–5 hours, or better still, overnight, until well chilled.

Recipe continues overleaf

Line two baking trays with baking paper.

Next, shape the buns: weigh the dough and divide it into 10 equal portions. Pinch a portion into a ball shape, then cup your hand over the dough and move your cupped hand in a quick, tight circular motion – this will cause the seam to come together and create tension on the surface of the dough. Repeat to shape all the buns and place them on the lined trays – no need to cover them at this point. Place the trays in the oven (with the oven switched off) and place a bowl of freshly boiled water on the floor of the oven. Close the oven door and leave the buns to rest for approximately 20 minutes. Remove the buns from the oven and leave for 5 minutes to dry a little.

Now fill the buns with raspberry cream. To do this, hold a bun with floured hands and turn it, like a steering wheel, as well as stretching at the same time to form a disc, being careful not to remove too much air. Place it on your lightly floured work surface, seam-side facing up. Spoon 1–1½ teaspoons of the raspberry cream in the centre of the disc; take care not to overfill, or else your buns will explode. Pull up the sides and pinch them together at the top to seal. You do not need to do anything else to shape the buns at this point! This will only create weak spots where the filling can run out during baking. Place the filled bun, seam-side down, on a lined baking sheet and repeat to fill the rest of the buns. Cover with a lightly dampened dish towel and leave to prove for 40 minutes–1 hour, or until the buns have doubled in size.

Towards the end of the proving time, preheat the oven to 190°C fan (410°C), gas 6, and whisk together the ingredients for the egg wash. Brush the buns with egg wash. Bake for 12–13 minutes, or until golden brown and hollow sounding when tapped on the base. Leave to cool on a wire rack.

Once the buns are cool, prepare the chocolate topping. Put the butter and water in a small saucepan over a low heat until the butter has melted. Add the chocolate and heat for another 30–60 seconds until the chocolate has melted. Remove from the heat and stir until smooth and well combined. Pour into a deep bowl and leave to cool for 10–15 minutes.

Stir the chocolate topping, then dip the top of each bun into it. Sprinkle with freeze-dried raspberry pieces and leave for 20–30 minutes so the icing sets a little. Best eaten on the day of baking.

EARL GREY HOT CROSS BUNS

These old favourites are steeped in Earl Grey – which adds a lovely fragrance and flavour – then spruced up with a sweet orange glaze. A piping bag is useful for this recipe.

MAKES 9 BUNS | **VO** (see page 153)

2 Earl Grey tea bags
130g (4½oz) just-boiled water
55g (2oz) sultanas (golden raisins)
55g (2oz) raisins
1 recipe quantity Tangzhong Method Dough (see page 34), made with reference to the method here
1½ tsp Mixed Spice Blend (see page 74)
1 tsp ground cinnamon
finely grated zest of 1 small orange
30g (1oz) mixed candied peel
strong white bread flour, for dusting

EGG WASH
1 large egg
1 tsp water
a pinch of fine sea salt

CROSS
45g (1½oz) plain (all-purpose) flour
55g (2oz) milk

ORANGE GLAZE
3 tbsp orange juice
3 tbsp golden caster (granulated) sugar

Use one of the Earl Grey tea bags and the hot water to brew some tea. Put the sultanas and raisins in a bowl, pour over the freshly brewed tea and leave to soak for 30 minutes. Once the time is up, drain through a sieve.

Heat the 145g (5oz) milk (from the second part of the tangzhong dough recipe on page 34) to boiling, then remove from the heat, add the other tea bag and leave to steep for 4 minutes. Squeeze out and discard the bag, then let the milk cool to room temperature. Once cooled, weigh and if it's less than 145g (5oz), add a dash more milk to make it up to this weight.

Make the tangzhong dough recipe following the directions on pages 34–7, using the tea-infused milk and adding the mixed spice blend, cinnamon and orange zest into the flour in step 2, then proceed as instructed. Once the dough has reached the windowpane stage, add the pre-soaked fruit and candied peel. Knead for 1–2 minutes to incorporate the fruit. Turn out onto the work surface and scoop up any stray fruit and add to the dough. Place in a bowl and cover. Either place in the fridge overnight (up to 12 hours) or prove in a warm spot for 1–1½ hours, or until doubled in size – this will depend on the room temperature.

Recipe continues overleaf

Line a baking tray with baking paper.

Knock back the dough, then weigh it and divide into 9 equal portions. To shape the buns, add a very small amount of flour to the work surface, then place your cupped hand over a portion of the dough. Move your cupped hand in a quick, tight circular motion – this will cause the seam to come together and create tension on the surface of the dough and make the bun perfectly round. Repeat to shape all the buns, then arrange them in a square shape on the baking tray, leaving enough space between them for the dough to expand. Cover with a lightly dampened dish towel and leave to prove for 1–1½ hours, depending on the room temperature, until doubled in size.

Towards the end of the proving time, preheat the oven to 180°C (400°C), gas 6.

Brush each bun with the egg wash.

To make the paste for the cross, mix the flour with the milk. Spoon it into a piping bag with a 5mm (¼ inch) round nozzle (or make a baking paper piping bag). Pipe a line along each row of buns, then repeat in the other direction to create crosses.

Bake the buns in the preheated oven for approximately 20–22 minutes, or until they turn golden brown.

While they bake, make the orange glaze: combine the orange juice and sugar, in a small saucepan and simmer gently until it thickens a little. Brush the surface of each bun with the glaze when they come out of the oven. Leave to cool completely on the wire rack.

Best eaten on the day, or the day after baking. Store in an airtight container, or freeze on the day of baking for up to 3 months. Once defrosted, slice in half and toast lightly.

ELDERFLOWER & STRAWBERRY

There are a few elements that make up this bun, but it's so worth it. Do note that some elements are best made the day before. It's all about the different tastes and textures here – soft, airy crumb, creamy elderflower-infused custard and sweet summer strawberries. It encapsulates the essence of summer. A piping bag is useful for this recipe. Pictured on pages 90–1.

MAKES 10 BUNS

1 recipe quantity Basic Enriched Dough (see page 26)
strong white bread flour, for dusting
120g ($4\frac{1}{4}$oz) fresh strawberries, sliced

ELDERFLOWER CUSTARD
225g (8oz) full-fat milk
3 egg yolks (about 55–60g/2oz)
25g (1oz) elderflower cordial
35g ($1\frac{1}{4}$oz) caster (granulated) sugar
12g ($\frac{1}{2}$oz) cornflour (cornstarch)
10g ($\frac{1}{3}$oz) unsalted butter, cold and diced

STRAWBERRY COMPOTE
175g (6oz) fresh strawberries
25g (1oz) elderflower cordial
$2\frac{1}{2}$ tsp cornflour (cornstarch)
40g ($1\frac{1}{2}$oz) golden caster (granulated) sugar

VANILLA BUTTER FILLING
60g ($2\frac{1}{4}$oz) unsalted butter, softened
35g ($1\frac{1}{4}$oz) caster (granulated) sugar
1 tsp Vanilla Sugar (see page 150)

EGG WASH
1 large egg
1 tsp water
a pinch of fine sea salt

ELDERFLOWER SYRUP
6 tbsp elderflower cordial
1 tbsp golden caster (granulated) sugar

TIP: If you're keen to use fresh elderflowers instead of cordial, use 2–3 elderflower heads, shaken to remove any bugs.

Begin with the elderflower custard – this is ideally made a day ahead of baking the buns. Bring the milk to a simmer in a small saucepan. In a mixing bowl, beat together the egg yolks, cordial, sugar and cornflour until pale and fluffy. Pour the hot milk in a steady stream into the egg mixture, whisking continuously. Pour the mixture back into the saucepan and heat, beating all the time until it thickens and boils. Pour the custard into a cold bowl and stir in the butter, beating until it is completely incorporated. Place a piece of baking paper directly on the surface of the custard to stop a skin forming, and leave to cool. Transfer to the fridge when cool.

The strawberry compote is also best made the day before. Blitz the strawberries, elderflower cordial, cornflour and sugar until smooth. Pour into a small saucepan and bring to the boil, whisking as it thickens. Pour into a bowl, cool, cover and place in the fridge.

For the fiilling, mix the softened butter with the sugar and vanilla sugar to a smooth paste. Set aside.

Line two baking trays with baking paper.

Knock back the dough. On a lightly floured work surface, roll out the prepared dough to a rectangle measuring approximately 54 x 30cm (20¾ x 12 inches), lifting it a few times during rolling to release the tension in the dough. Spread the vanilla butter evenly over the dough with an offset spatula. With a short edge towards you, fold the dough in three, folding the bottom third up to cover the middle and the top third down to cover that. Gently roll out the dough again to a rectangle measuring 17 x 35cm (6½ x 14 inches).

With a pizza roller or large knife, cut the dough into 10 wide strips, each measuring approximately 35mm (1½ inches) across. Cut along the length of a strip through the middle, almost to the top (it should look like a pair of trousers). Now twist the two strands of dough in different directions, twisting one clockwise and the other anti-clockwise, then tie them in a knot. Repeat to shape all the buns. Some of the filling will escape, so rinse your hands between each shaping. Once shaped, place the buns on the lined baking sheets. Cover with a lightly dampened dish towel and leave them to prove for about 1–1½ hours, or until doubled in size.

Towards the end of the proving time, preheat the oven to 190°C fan (410°C), gas 6, and whisk together all the ingredients for the egg wash.

Using a handheld electric whisk, beat the custard until it's smooth. Spoon into a piping bag, fitted with a plain 1cm (½ inch) nozzle. Give the strawberry compote a stir, then spoon it into another piping bag fitted with a plain 1cm (½ inch) nozzle.

Brush the buns with the egg wash. Pipe a little strawberry compote into one side of each bun, and elderflower custard into the other. Top the compote-filled sides with a slice of strawberry. Bake for 10–12 minutes, or until golden.

While the buns are baking, make the elderflower syrup. In a small saucepan, gently heat the elderflower cordial and sugar until the sugar has dissolved, then remove from the heat. When the buns are ready, brush with a little syrup and leave to cool on a wire rack. Best eaten on the day of baking.

FESTIVE SPICED BUNS

There's no aroma that reminds me more of the festive season quite like freshly baked *pepparkakor* (ginger thins). These Swedish spiced buns are so irresistible that it's impossible to stop at just one. In this recipe, I've used the same aromatic spice blend as in traditional *pepparkakor*, combining cinnamon, ginger, cloves, cardamom and a little black pepper.

MAKES 10 BUNS | **VO** (see page 153)

1 recipe quantity Basic Enriched Dough (see page 26)
strong white bread flour, for dusting
Sugar Syrup (see page 148)
30g (1oz) sugar nibs

FILLING
90g (3¼oz) unsalted butter, softened
2 tsp ground cinnamon
1 tsp ground ginger
1 tsp freshly ground cardamom
¼ tsp ground cloves
a few twists of freshly ground black pepper
1 tbsp black treacle
40g (1½oz) icing (confectioners') sugar

EGG WASH
1 large egg
1 tsp water
a pinch of fine sea salt

Begin with the filling: in a small bowl and using a rubber spatula, blend the butter, spices, black treacle and sugar. Set aside.

Line two baking trays with baking paper.

Knock back the dough. On a lightly floured work surface, roll the dough out to a rectangle measuring 52 x 28cm (20¾ x 11¼ inches), lifting it a few times during rolling to release the tension in the dough. Spread the spiced butter all over the surface of the dough with an offset spatula. With a short edge towards you, fold the dough in three, folding the bottom third up to cover the middle and the top third down to cover that. Do a quarter turn so that the seams are at the top and bottom, then gently roll out the dough again to a rectangle measuring approximately 36 x 20cm (14¼ x 8 inches).

With a pizza roller or large knife, cut the dough into 10 even strips along the short edge, each 2cm (¾ inch) wide. Now coil a strip into a spiral, tucking the end under to stop it unravelling while baking. Repeat to shape all the buns and place them on the lined baking trays, making sure they have space to expand. Cover with a lightly dampened dish towel and leave to prove for 1–1½ hours, or until doubled in size.

Towards the end of the proving time, preheat the oven to 190°C fan (410°C), gas 6, and whisk together the ingredients for the egg wash.

Brush the buns with egg wash. Bake for 10–12 minutes, or until golden brown. As soon as they come out of the oven, brush with sugar syrup and shower with sugar nibs. Leave to cool on a wire rack.

These are best eaten on the day of baking, however they freeze incredibly well for up to 3 months. Once defrosted, just warm them in a medium oven for 5–8 minutes.

HAZELNUT BUTTER & DATE

I have a weakness for Medjool dates, which are soft dates with a natural, caramel-like sweetness. Blended with nuts, they make a great filling for a bun. Use whatever nuts you fancy – cashews are a great alternative. Pictured on pages 96–7.

MAKES 10 BUNS | **VO** (see page 153)

1 recipe quantity Basic Enriched Dough (see page 26)
strong white bread flour, for dusting
Sugar Syrup (see page 148)

FILLING
110g (3¾oz) blanched hazelnuts
7 soft Medjool dates (about 120g/4¼oz), chopped
60g (2¼oz) just-boiled water

EGG WASH
1 large egg
1 tsp water
a pinch of fine sea salt

Begin with the filling: preheat the oven to 180°C fan (400°C), gas 6 and tip the hazelnuts onto a lipped baking tray. Roast for 8–10 minutes until golden, then set aside to cool. Reserve 20g (¾oz) for decorating the bun and blend the rest of the nuts in a food processor until they form a creamy butter. They will go from whole to crumbs, then clumps, and finally to a smooth nut butter consistency. This can take anywhere from 5 to 8 minutes. Now add the dates and boiling water and blend until smooth. Set aside.

Line two baking trays with baking paper.

Knock back the dough. On a lightly floured work surface, roll the dough out to a rectangle measuring 75 x 24cm (30 x 9½ inches), lifting it a few times during rolling to release the tension in the dough. Spread the butter for the filling evenly over the dough with an offset spatula. With a short edge towards you, fold the dough in three, folding the bottom third up to cover the middle and the top third down to cover that – making sure the seams meet. Gently roll out the dough again to a rectangle measuring 25 x 28cm (10 x 11 inches).

With a pizza roller or large knife, cut the dough into 10 even strips along the short edge, each 2.5cm (1 inch) wide, then cut each strip in half lengthways. Place a dough strip on the work surface and brush the dough lightly with a little water. Place another one on top. Turn the sandwiched strip on its side, so that the cut-sides are up and you can see the filling, then take both ends and stretch them a little. Coil the top of the strip into the middle on one side and coil the bottom of the strip up on the other side in the other direction to make a figure of eight, then press the bun down gently to flatten it out. Cover with a lightly dampened dish towel and leave to prove for 1–1½ hours, or until the dough springs back when you press your finger gently into it.

Towards the end of the proving time, preheat the oven to 190°C fan (410°C), gas 6, and chop the reserved hazelnuts. Whisk together all the ingredients for the egg wash.

Brush the buns with the egg wash and sprinkle with the chopped hazelnuts. Bake for 10–12 minutes, or until golden. When they are ready, brush with a little syrup and leave to cool on a wire rack. Best eaten on the day of baking.

LEMON & POPPY SEED

Every bite of this bright and zesty bun captures the essence of a sunny day. I could not live without lemons; they perk up any dish. I frequently incorporate lemon curd into buttercreams or frostings for my cakes. You'll have more lemon curd than you need for this recipe, but it keeps well if jarred.

MAKES 10 BUNS

1 recipe quantity Basic Enriched Dough (see page 26)
strong white bread flour, for dusting
icing (confectioners') sugar, for dusting
125g ($4\frac{1}{2}$oz) Lemon Curd (see below)

LEMON CURD
finely grated zest of 2 unwaxed lemons
120g ($4\frac{1}{4}$oz) freshly squeezed lemon juice
80g ($2\frac{3}{4}$oz) unsalted butter, cut into cubes
100g ($3\frac{1}{2}$oz) unrefined granulated sugar
3 free-range eggs

FILLING
90g ($3\frac{1}{4}$oz) unsalted butter, softened
40g ($4\frac{1}{2}$oz) icing (confectioners') sugar, plus extra for dusting
2 tbsp poppy seeds
$1\frac{1}{2}$ tsp Vanilla Sugar (see page 150)

EGG WASH
1 large egg
1 tsp water
a pinch of fine sea salt

Recipe continues overleaf

Begin with the lemon curd; you can make this well in advance. Combine the lemon zest and juice, butter and sugar in a heatproof bowl. Place the bowl over a saucepan of gently simmering water, ensuring it fits snugly without touching the water. Stir the mixture lightly from time to time until the butter begins to melt, making sure the temperature of the mixture does not exceed 50°C (122°F). In the meantime, beat the eggs in a small bowl. Pour a third of the lemon mixture over the eggs and whisk, then pour the egg mixture back into the remaining lemon mixture. Whisk briskly with a balloon whisk for about a minute until well combined. Continue to cook the mixture for 9–10 minutes, scraping the sides occasionally with a spatula and whisking continuously. The curd is ready when it is thick, glossy on the surface, and the temperature reaches 78–80°C (172–176°F). Remove from the heat and strain through a fine sieve. Transfer the curd to two sterilized jars and seal them immediately. Store the jars in a cool place for up to 4 weeks. Once opened, refrigerate and consume within 2 weeks. This will freeze well, too.

For the filling, in a small bowl with a rubber spatula, blend the butter, icing sugar, poppy seeds and vanilla sugar. Set aside.

Line two baking trays with baking paper.

Knock back the dough. On a lightly floured work surface, roll out the dough to a rectangle measuring 54 x 30cm (20¾ x 12 inches), lifting it a few times during rolling to release the tension in the dough. Spread the poppy seed filling all over the surface of the dough with an offset spatula. With a short edge towards you, fold the dough in three, folding the bottom third up to cover the middle and the top third down to cover that. Gently roll out the dough again to a rectangle measuring 17 x 35cm (6½ x 14 inches).

With a pizza roller or large knife, cut the dough into 10 wide strips, each measuring approximately 35mm (1½ inches) across. Cut along the length of a strip through the middle, almost to the top (it should look like a pair of trousers). Now twist the two strands of dough in different directions, twisting one clockwise and the other anti-clockwise, then tie them in a knot. Repeat to shape all the buns. Place the buns on the lined baking sheets. Cover with a lightly dampened dish towel and leave to prove for 1–1½ hours, or until approximately doubled in size.

Towards the end of the proving time, preheat the oven to 190°C fan (410°C), gas 6, and whisk together the ingredients for the egg wash.

Brush the buns with egg wash. Gently make an indentation in the centre of each bun with a teaspoon, then place a teaspoonful of lemon curd in each indentation. Bake for 10–12 minutes, or until golden brown. Leave to cool on a wire rack. Dust with icing sugar.

Best eaten on the day of baking, however, they freeze incredibly well. Once defrosted, just warm them in a medium oven for 5–8 minutes.

MOCHA & SEA SALT

Delicious served warm from the oven for afternoon tea or when you are craving something indulgent, sweet and chocolatey. As an alternative to espresso powder in the chocolate ganache, you could add ½ teaspoon of ground ginger to the cream, or infuse the cream with orange zest (see tip below). Pictured on pages 104–105.

MAKES 10 BUNS

1 recipe quantity Tangzhong Method Dough (see page 34)
strong white bread flour, for dusting
cocoa powder, for dusting
sea salt flakes, for sprinkling

MOCHA GANACHE
75g (2½oz) double (heavy) cream
½ tsp espresso powder
150g (5½oz) good-quality milk chocolate (about 35% cocoa solids)

EGG WASH
1 large egg
1 tsp water
a pinch of fine sea salt

SUGAR SYRUP
1½ tbsp golden granulated sugar
1½ tbsp water

TIP: To infuse the cream with orange, zest a small orange and add the zest to the cream in a small saucepan. Gently heat, then set aside to infuse for 10 minutes. Pass through a fine sieve, then reheat and proceed with adding the chopped chocolate.

Begin with the mocha ganache: heat the cream and espresso powder in a small saucepan to just boiling, then remove from the heat. Add the chocolate and leave for a minute, then stir with a small rubber spatula until the chocolate has melted. Pour into a bowl and cover the surface directly with a disc of baking paper. Leave to cool to room temperature, then place in the fridge to set. Once completely set, divide into 10 equal portions and roll into balls. Place back in the fridge until needed.

Line two baking trays with baking paper.

Knock back the dough. Weigh the dough and divide it into 10 equal portions. To shape the buns, add a very small amount of flour to the work surface, then place your cupped hand over a portion of the dough. Move your cupped hand in a quick, tight circular motion – this will cause the seam to come together and create tension on the surface of the dough and make the bun perfectly round. Repeat to shape all the buns and place them on the lined trays – no need to cover them at this point. Place the trays in the oven (with the oven switched off) and place a bowl of freshly boiled water on the floor of the oven. Close the oven door and leave the buns to rest for approximately 20 minutes. Remove the buns from the oven and leave for 5 minutes to dry a little.

Now to shape the bun and fill with the mocha ganache. To do this, hold a bun with floured hands and turn it, like a steering wheel, as well as stretching at the same time to form a disc, being careful not to remove too much air. Place it on a lightly floured work surface, seam-side facing up. Place a mocha ball in the centre of the disc. Pull up the sides and pinch together at the top to seal. You do not need to do anything else to shape the buns at this point. This will only create weak spots where the filling may run out during baking. Place the filled bun, seam-side down, on the lined baking sheet and repeat to fill the rest of the buns. Cover with a lightly dampened dish towel and leave to prove for 40–60 minutes, or until the buns have doubled in size.

Towards the end of the proving time, preheat the oven to 190°C fan (410°C), gas 6, and whisk together the ingredients for the egg wash.

Brush the buns with egg wash. Bake for 12–14 minutes, or until golden brown and hollow sounding when tapped on the base. Leave to cool on a wire rack.

Brush with sugar syrup very sparingly. When the sugar syrup has cooled, dust lightly with cocoa and sprinkle a few sea salt flakes on each bun. Best eaten on the day of baking.

NORDIC CINNAMON BUNS

The aroma of cinnamon buns still takes me back to baking in my granny's kitchen when I was five. Sweet cinnamon swirls topped with crunchy sugar nibs, unravelling to the centre – the most delicious part. I approach the shaping of the bun differently now than I did back then, but the principle remains the same.

MAKES 10 BUNS | **VO** (see page 153)

1 recipe quantity Basic Enriched Dough (see page 26)
strong white bread flour, for dusting
30g (1oz) sugar nibs
freshly ground cardamom, for dusting
Sugar Syrup (see page 148), for brushing

FILLING
95g (3¼oz) unsalted butter, softened
45g (1½oz) golden caster (granulated) sugar
4 tsp ground cinnamon

EGG WASH
1 large egg
1 tsp water
a pinch of fine sea salt

Begin with the filling: in a small bowl and using a rubber spatula, blend the butter, sugar and cinnamon. Set aside.

Line two baking trays with baking paper.

Knock back the dough. On a lightly floured work surface, roll the dough out to a rectangle measuring 52 x 28cm (20¾ x 11¼ inches), lifting it a few times during rolling to release the tension in the dough. Spread the cinnamon butter all over the surface of the dough with an offset spatula. With a short edge towards you, fold the dough in three, folding the bottom third up to cover the middle and the top third down to cover that, making sure all the seams line up. Give the dough a quarter turn, so that the seams are at the top and bottom. Gently roll out again to a rectangle measuring approximately 36 x 20cm (14¼ x 8 inches).

With a pizza roller or large knife, cut the dough into strips, each 2cm (¾ inch) wide. Now coil a dough strip round on itself to make a circle, tucking the end under to stop it unravelling while baking. Repeat to shape the rest of the buns and place on the lined baking trays, leaving space between each bun. Cover with a lightly dampened dish towel and leave to prove for 1–1½ hours, or until approximately doubled in size.

Towards the end of the proving time, preheat the oven to 190°C fan (410°C), gas 6, and whisk together all the ingredients for the egg wash.

Brush the buns with the egg wash and shower with sugar nibs and a little ground cardamom. Bake for 10–12 minutes, or until golden brown. As soon as they come out of the oven, brush with sugar syrup. Cool on a wire rack. Best eaten on the day of baking, however, they freeze well for up to 3 months. Once defrosted, just warm them in a medium oven for 5–8 minutes.

ORANGE & FENNEL MARITOZZI

My first encounter with this incredible bun was on holiday in Rome a few years ago. Although the original recipe offers subtle hints of citrus, I wanted to complement that flavour by adding the perfect partner, fennel. You'll need to make the curd and let it set before you start baking the buns, but this can be done days, or even weeks, in advance, as can the candied fennel seeds.

MAKES 10 BUNS

1 recipe quantity Tangzhong Method Dough (see page 34)
strong white bread flour, for dusting
Orange and Fennel Curd (see below), for spreading
icing (confectioners') sugar, for dusting

ORANGE AND FENNEL CURD
120g (4¼oz) freshly squeezed orange juice (about 2 oranges)
1½ tbsp fennel seeds
2 tbsp lemon juice (optional, if your oranges are very sweet)
80g (2¾oz) unsalted butter, cut into small pieces
100g (3½oz) unrefined granulated sugar
3 large free-range eggs, plus 1 egg yolk
finely grated zest of 2 unwaxed oranges, plus a little extra to decorate

CANDIED FENNEL SEEDS
2 tbsp golden caster (granulated) sugar
2 tbsp water
2 tbsp fennel seeds

ORANGE CREAM FILLING
500g (17oz) double (heavy) cream
80g (2¾oz) Orange & Fennel Curd (see above)

EGG WASH
1 large egg
1 tsp water
a pinch of fine sea salt

Recipe continues overleaf

First, make the orange and fennel curd. Combine the orange juice, fennel seeds, lemon juice (if using), butter and sugar in a heatproof bowl. Place the bowl over a saucepan of gently simmering water, ensuring it fits snugly without touching the water. Stir the mixture lightly from time to time until the butter begins to melt, make sure the temperature does not exceed 50°C (122°F). In the meantime, beat the eggs and egg yolk in a separate bowl. Gradually pour the orange mixture over the eggs, whisking as you do so. Now pour the mixture back into the bowl set over the saucepan with simmering water. Whisk the mixture briskly with a balloon whisk for about a minute until well combined. Continue to cook the mixture for 9–10 minutes, scraping the sides occasionally with a spatula and whisking continuously. The curd is ready when it is thick, glossy, and the temperature reaches 78–80°C (172–176°F). Remove from the heat and strain through a fine sieve. Now add the orange zest. Transfer the curd to two sterilized jars and seal immediately. Store the jars in a cool place for up to 4 weeks. Once opened, refrigerate and consume within 2 weeks. This will freeze well, too.

To make the candied fennel seeds, combine the sugar and water in a small saucepan, then bring to the boil over a medium–high heat. Stir continuously until the mixture becomes syrupy, which typically takes about 2–3 minutes and will produce a lot more bubbles. Reduce the heat to medium and add the fennel seeds. Keep stirring until the mixture crystallizes; this will happen suddenly, and the fennel seeds will appear almost dry. Quickly remove from the heat and continue stirring for a few more seconds until the fennel seeds are dry and separated. They will look a little like breadcrumbs. Transfer to a sealable, airtight container – they will keep for several weeks. Line two baking trays with baking paper.

For the buns, knock back the dough, then weigh and divide it into 10 equal pieces. To shape the buns, add a very small amount of flour to the work surface, then place your cupped hand over a portion of the dough. Move your cupped hand in a quick, tight circular motion – this will cause the seam to come together and create tension on the surface of the dough and make the bun perfectly round. Repeat to shape all the buns and place on the lined baking sheet. Cover with a lightly dampened dish towel and leave to prove for 1–1½ hours, or until doubled in size.

Towards the end of the proving time, preheat the oven to 190°C fan (410°C), gas 6, and whisk together the ingredients for the egg wash.

Brush the buns with egg wash and bake for 10–13 minutes, or until golden and when you tap the base of the buns they sound hollow. Leave to cool on a wire rack.

Meanwhile, make the orange cream filling. In a medium bowl, using a handheld electric mixer or a balloon whisk, beat the cream and orange and fennel curd on high until soft peaks form – approximately 1 minute.

Using a serrated knife, make a cut in each bun at an angle. Don't cut all the way through – it should be like a hot dog bun. Open the buns as wide as you can without splitting them. Spread 1 teaspoon of orange curd on each cut-side of the buns. Now generously pipe or spoon the whipped cream into the buns. Smooth off with a dinner knife or spatula and dust with icing sugar. Top the cream with a little orange zest and candied fennel seeds.

Serve the maritozzi immediately or refrigerate for up to 6 hours. If refrigerated, remove 20 minutes before serving to allow the buns to soften.

PISTACHIO & PEACH

I recently bought a jar of smooth pistachio nut butter on impulse – I knew it would be one of those handy ingredients that'd be an excellent addition to desserts, buttercreams and salad dressings, and I wasn't wrong. Use firm peaches; if they're too ripe, they'll just collapse when roasted. A piping bag is useful for this recipe.

MAKES 10 BUNS

1 recipe quantity Tangzhong Method Dough (see page 34)
strong white bread flour, for dusting
20g (3/4oz) pistachios, finely chopped

PISTACHIO CREAM
50g (1 3/4oz) smooth pistachio butter
35g (1 1/4oz) icing (confectioners') sugar
170g (6oz) mascarpone cheese
125g (4 1/2oz) double (heavy) cream

ROASTED PEACHES
3 donut peaches
1 tbsp brown sugar
1 tbsp honey
1 tbsp lemon thyme leaves (use standard thyme if you can't find lemon thyme)
2 tbsp water

EGG WASH
1 large egg
1 tsp water
a pinch of fine sea salt

For the pistachio cream: put the pistachio butter in a medium bowl, add the icing sugar and mascarpone and whisk until smooth. In a separate bowl, whip the cream to soft peaks, then fold the cream into the pistachio butter mixture. Cover and place in the fridge.

Preheat the oven to 190°C fan (410°C), gas 6. Cut the peaches in half and remove the stones. Cut each half into thirds and place them, cut-sides up, in a baking dish. Sprinkle each piece with brown sugar, honey and lemon thyme leaves and add the 2 tablespoons of water to the baking dish. Roast for 15 minutes, or until the peaches have softened and caramelized a little – they should still hold their shape. Set aside to cool.

Line two baking trays with baking paper.

Knock back the dough, then weigh the dough and divide it into 10 equal portions. To shape the buns, add a very small amount of flour to the work surface, then place your cupped hand over a portion of the dough. Move your cupped hand in a quick, tight circular motion – this will cause the seam to come together and create tension on the surface of the dough and make the bun perfectly round. Repeat to shape all the buns. Place the buns on the baking sheet. Cover with a lightly dampened dish towel and leave to prove for 1–1 1/2 hours depending on the room temperature, or until doubled in size.

Towards the end of the proving time, preheat the oven to 190°C fan (410°C), gas 6, and whisk together the egg wash ingredients.

Egg wash the buns and bake for 12–14 minutes, or until golden and hollow sounding when tapped on the base. Leave to cool on a wire rack.

With a serrated knife, cut a 1cm (1/2in) hole in the top of each bun and hollow out a little of the crumb. Spoon the pistachio cream into a piping bag fitted with a 1cm (1/2 inch) round nozzle. Pipe the filling into each bun, finishing with a swirl on the top. Make an indentation in the cream with a warm teaspoon and add a slice of peach, and a little of the roasting liquor. Sprinkle with the chopped pistachios. Best eaten on the day of baking.

PISTACHIO, LIME & ROSE

These buns are zingy and citrusy. The sharpness of the lime pairs so well with the rich pistachio butter, while rose petals are added sparingly to enhance the flavours without overpowering them.

MAKES 10 BUNS | **VO** (see page 153)

1 recipe quantity Basic Enriched Dough (see page 26)
strong white bread flour, for dusting
25g (1oz) unsalted pistachio nuts, chopped

FILLING
45g (1½oz) unsalted pistachio nuts
70g (2½oz) unsalted butter
55g (2oz) caster (granulated) sugar
20g (¾oz) ground almonds
zest of 1½ limes

EGG WASH
1 large egg
1 tsp water
a pinch of fine sea salt

LIME SYRUP
2 tbsp lime juice
2 tbsp sugar
a few dried rose petals

Begin with the filling: blitz the pistachios in a high-speed blender to a fine meal, or very finely chop with a knife. Combine with the remaining filling ingredients and set aside.

Line two baking trays with baking paper.

Knock back the dough. On a lightly floured work surface, roll out the dough to a rectangle measuring 75 x 25cm (30 x 10 inches), lifting it a few times during rolling to release the tension in the dough. Spread the pistachio butter all over the surface of the dough with an offset spatula. Fold the dough in half, making sure the seams line up. Gently roll out again to a rectangle measuring approximately 40 x 25cm (16 x 10 inches).

Using a pizza roller or large knife, cut the dough into 10 strips along the short edge of the rectangle, each roughly 25mm (1 inch) wide. Twist a strip into a spiral, then place it on the work surface and coil it around itself to form a pinwheel shape. Place on a lined baking sheet and tuck the end under to stop it unravelling when baking. Repeat to shape the rest of the buns, leaving a little space between each bun on the trays for them to expand. Cover with a lightly dampened dish towel and prove for 1–1½ hours or until approximately doubled in size.

Towards the end of the proving time, preheat the oven to 190°C fan (410°C), gas 6, and whisk together the ingredients for the egg wash.

Brush the buns with egg wash and shower with the chopped pistachios. Bake for 10–12 minutes, or until golden brown.

While the buns are baking, make the lime syrup. Bring all the syrup ingredients to a slow boil in a small saucepan. When the buns are ready, brush with a little syrup and leave to cool on a wire rack.

Best eaten on the day of baking or they freeze well. Once defrosted, warm through in a medium oven for 5–8 minutes.

PRALINE & DOUBLE ESPRESSO

A light and airy praline bun, kicked up with a good dose of espresso. If you don't have a coffee machine, simply make up the espresso using instant espresso powder.

MAKES 10 BUNS

1 recipe quantity Tangzhong Method Dough (see page 34), with 1½ tbsp freshly ground cardamom added to the flour in step 2
strong white bread flour, for dusting
ground coffee, for sprinkling
icing (confectioners') sugar, for dusting

HAZELNUT PRALINE PASTE
175g (6oz) blanched hazelnuts
95g (3¼oz) white granulated or caster sugar
¼ tsp fine sea salt
1½–2 tbsp espresso
40g (1½oz) full-fat milk

EGG WASH
1 large egg
1 tsp water
a pinch of fine sea salt

WHIPPED ESPRESSO CREAM
280g (10oz) double (heavy) cream
1 tbsp cold espresso
15g (½oz) Vanilla Sugar (see page 150)

TIP: These are also delicious with 1½ tablespoons of freshly ground cardamom added to the dough.

Begin with the praline. Preheat the oven to 180°C fan (400°C), gas 6, and tip all the hazelnuts onto a lipped baking tray. Roast for 8–10 minutes until golden, then set aside to cool. Once cool, remove 25g (1oz) of the nuts from the tray, roughly chop them and set aside for decorating.

For the next bit, have a baking tray lined with baking paper ready, sitting on a wooden chopping board.

Put the sugar in a shallow stainless steel pan. It should be in a thin layer for best results; the wider the pan, the faster the sugar will melt and caramelize. Heat over a medium heat. After a few minutes, the sugar will begin to melt at the edges. Gently move the sugar around in the pan using a spatula and shake the pan so that the unmelted sugar can come into contact with the bottom of the pan. Keep cooking while gently swirling the pan to melt the sugar. It's extremely hot, so take care. The sugar will quickly go from a colourless liquid to golden. Do not leave the sugar unattended as this process will happen quickly and you need to keep an eye on it. As soon as the sugar turns a light amber colour, remove the pan from the heat and carefully pour the sugar onto the lined baking tray. The caramel will darken a little from the residual heat. Set aside to cool.

Recipe continues overleaf

Once the caramel is cool and hard, break it into smaller pieces. Place the pieces in the bowl of your food processor or high-speed blender. Add the roasted nuts and the salt and blitz until everything is very finely chopped. Process the mixture for about 3–5 minutes, using a spatula to scrape the bottom and sides of the food processor occasionally so everything gets blended evenly. Alternatively, you can use a pestle and mortar. The praline paste will go through several stages. You're looking for a smooth paste that's still quite thick. Store in a jar in the fridge. This can be made several days ahead if you wish.

Line a baking sheet with baking paper.

Knock back the dough. Weigh and divide the dough into 10 equal pieces. To shape the buns, add a very small amount of flour to the work surface, then place your cupped hand over a portion of the dough. Roll the dough in a circular motion until it's perfectly round. Repeat to shape all the buns and place on the lined baking sheet. Cover with a lightly dampened dish towel and leave to prove for 1–1½ hours, or until doubled in size.

Towards the end of the proving time, preheat the oven to 190°C fan (410°C), gas 6, and whisk together the ingredients for the egg wash.

Brush the buns with egg wash and bake for 12–14 minutes, or until golden and when you tap the base of the buns they sound hollow. Leave to cool on a wire rack.

Once the buns have cooled, cut a hole in the top of each bun with a small serrated knife and hollow out a little of the crumb. You're looking to remove about 5g (⅛oz) from each bun. Keep the crumb.

Now add the espresso to the hazelnut praline – it will thicken and that's fine. Place the praline in a bowl with the bun crumb, add half of the milk, and stir. You want a thick paste that's not too runny. Add a little more milk, if needed, to form a paste. Set aside.

For the espresso cream, whip the cream with the espresso and vanilla sugar until stiff peaks form. Make sure you don't add more espresso than stated in the recipe, as there is a limit to how much espresso you can add to double cream before it becomes unwhippable.

To assemble, spoon some hazelnut praline paste into each bun, then spoon the espresso cream on the top. Sprinkle with the chopped nuts and a little ground coffee and dust with icing sugar. Best eaten on the day of baking.

RASPBERRY & HIBISCUS

Hibiscus flowers create a delicious floral and sharp flavour, making this an ideal breakfast bun. I've used raspberries for their taste and bright pink colour, but plums work just as well. Hibiscus powder is readily available online, but if you can't find it, grind dried hibiscus flowers as an alternative.

MAKES 12 BUNS | **VO** (see page 153)

1 recipe quantity Basic Enriched Dough (see page 26)
strong white bread flour, for dusting
icing (confectioners') sugar, for dusting

RASPBERRY AND HIBISCUS JAM
250g (9oz) frozen raspberries
1 tsp hibiscus powder
175g (6oz) golden granulated sugar
1 tbsp lemon juice

EGG WASH
1 large egg
1 tsp water
a pinch of fine sea salt

Begin with the raspberry and hibiscus jam, which is best made a day ahead of baking the buns. Put the raspberries, hibiscus powder, sugar and lemon juice in a medium saucepan. Bring to the boil, then simmer for approximately 8–10 minutes until the raspberries have broken down and the mixture is thick. Store in the fridge until needed.

Line two baking trays with baking paper.

Knock back the dough and divide into two equal pieces. On a lightly floured work surface, roll out a portion into a disc, 25cm (10 inches) in diameter, lifting it a few times during rolling to release the tension in the dough. Cut the disc into six equal triangles. Repeat to make six triangles from the second portion of dough.

To shape the crescents, start by rolling out each triangle widthways to get a little more surface area. Place 1–1½ teaspoons of jam at the widest end of a triangle, then proceed to roll the dough up. Making sure the pointed end is tucked underneath, turn the ends inwards to make a croissant shape. If a little filling escapes, it doesn't matter. Repeat to roll all the buns, then place on the lined baking trays, making sure there's space between the buns for them to expand. Cover with a lightly dampened dish towel and leave to prove for 1–1½ hours, or until the dough springs back when you press your finger gently into it.

Towards the end of the proving time, preheat the oven to 190°C fan (410°C), gas 6, and whisk together the ingredients for the egg wash.

Brush the crescents with egg wash. Bake for 8–10 minutes, or until golden brown. Leave to cool on a wire rack, then dust with icing sugar.

Best eaten on the day of baking, however they freeze incredibly well. Once defrosted, just warm them in a medium oven for 5–8 minutes.

RHUBARB, GINGER & CUSTARD

This is a classic flavour pairing. Forced rhubarb is my first choice here; I love the vibrant pink hue. However, young tender garden stems, picked in spring, will be lovely too. Adding 2–3 frozen raspberries to the compote while its cooking will help enhance the pink colour if the stems are particularly green. A piping bag is useful for this recipe.

MAKES 10 BUNS

1 recipe quantity Tangzhong Method Dough (see page 34)
strong white bread flour, for dusting
1 recipe quantity Vanilla Custard (see page 150)
icing (confectioners') sugar, for dusting

RHUBARB AND GINGER COMPOTE
300g (10½oz) forced or young rhubarb
50g (1¾oz) caster (granulated) sugar
1½ tbsp finely chopped stem ginger, plus 1½ tbsp of ginger syrup from the jar
1 tbsp water
3–4 frozen raspberries (optional)

EGG WASH
1 large egg
1 tsp water
a pinch of fine sea salt

Start with the rhubarb, which is ideally made a day ahead. Cut the rhubarb into 3cm (1¼ inch) pieces. Put them in a medium saucepan and add the sugar, ginger, ginger syrup and water. If the rhubarb is a little green, add a few raspberries to help with the colour. Simmer gently for 5–8 minutes, or until the rhubarb has almost broken down, but there is still a little texture. Set aside to cool completely.

Line two baking trays with baking paper.

Knock back the dough, weigh and divide it into 10 equal pieces. Add a very small amount of flour to the work surface, then place your cupped hand over a portion of the dough. Move your cupped hand in a quick, tight circular motion until you have a perfectly round bun. Using a rolling pin, roll the bun into a flat disc, approximately 2.5cm (1 inch) thick. Repeat with the other buns and place onto the lined baking trays. Cover with a lightly dampened dish towel and leave to prove for 1–1½ hours or until well risen and when you lightly press your finger into the dough, it springs back.

Towards the end of the proving time, preheat the oven to 190°C fan (410°C), gas 6, and whisk together the ingredients for the egg wash.

With a balloon whisk or a hand-held electric whisk, beat the vanilla custard until smooth. Spoon the custard into a piping bag fitted with a 1cm (½ inch) plain nozzle.

Once the buns have doubled in size, brush them with egg wash. Insert the piping bag nozzle into the centre of each bun and pipe a little of the custard into the bun, then finish with a swirl on the top. Bake for 10–12 minutes, or until golden brown.

Once the buns have cooled, add a generous teaspoonful of rhubarb and ginger compote to the top of each bun, then dust with icing sugar. Best eaten on the day of baking.

SAFFRON, ALMOND & ORANGE

Despite being the world's most expensive spice, saffron is widely used in Swedish baking, particularly around Christmas time in *saffransbullar*. Fortunately, only a small amount is needed to flavour the dough. If you haven't tried it before, saffron has a uniquely floral, slightly sweet and subtly earthy flavour, with hints of honey and hay.

MAKES 10 BUNS | **VO** (see page 153)

1 recipe quantity Basic Enriched Dough (see page 26), made with reference to the method here
a good pinch (about 1 x 0.5g pack) saffron threads
½ tsp sugar
strong white bread flour, for dusting
sugar nibs, to sprinkle
flaked (slivered) almonds, to sprinkle

FILLING
65g (2¼oz) unsalted butter, softened
80g (2¾oz) Almond Paste (see page 149), broken into small pieces
finely grated zest of 1 small unwaxed orange
1 tbsp icing (confectioners') sugar, plus extra for dusting

EGG WASH
1 large egg
1 tsp water
a pinch of fine sea salt

To start the dough, grind the saffron in a pestle and mortar with the ½ teaspoon sugar, then tip it into a small bowl. Warm the milk from the dough recipe in a small saucepan, then pour the warm milk over the saffron and sugar and stir. Allow to cool to room temperature, then proceed with the dough recipe as instructed.

For the filling: using an electric hand whisk or balloon whisk, blend the butter, almond paste, orange zest and icing sugar. Set aside.

Line two baking trays with baking paper.

Knock back the dough. On a lightly floured work surface, roll out the dough to a rectangle measuring 54 x 30cm (20¾ x 12 inches). Spread the almond butter all over the surface of the dough with an offset spatula. With a short edge towards you, fold the dough in three, folding the bottom third up to cover the middle and the top third down to cover that. Gently roll out the dough again to a rectangle measuring 17 x 35cm (6½ x 14 inches).

Cut the dough into 10 even strips along the short edge, each 2cm (¾ inch) wide. Twist a strip several times to make a spiral. Now wrap it round your index and middle finger, and put the end through the gap between your fingers. (This will prevent it unravelling when it bakes). Repeat to shape all the buns, placing them on the lined baking trays as you go, leaving space between each for the dough to expand. Cover with a lightly dampened dish towel and leave to prove for 1–1½ hours or until approximately doubled in size.

Towards the end of the proving time, preheat the oven to 190°C fan (410°C), gas 6, and whisk together the ingredients for the egg wash.

Brush the buns with egg wash and shower with sugar nibs and almonds. Bake for 10–12 minutes, or until golden brown. Leave to cool on a wire rack. Dust with a little icing sugar if desired.

Best eaten on the day of baking, however, they freeze well. Once defrosted, just warm through in a medium oven for 6–8 minutes.

SCHOOL BUNS

Norwegian school buns, known as *skolleboller*, are filled with creamy vanilla custard and coated in coconut. I would have been thrilled to eat one of these buns during a school break!

MAKES 10 BUNS

1 recipe quantity Tangzhong Method Dough (see page 34), with 1 tbsp freshly ground cardamom added at stage 2
strong white bread flour, for dusting
1 recipe quantity Vanilla Custard (see page 150)

COATING
90g (3¼oz) icing (confectioners') sugar
2–3 tsp water
60g (2¼oz) desiccated (dried shredded) coconut

Line two baking trays with baking paper.

Knock back the dough and divide it into 10 equal pieces. To shape the buns, add a very small amount of flour to the work surface, then place your cupped hand over a portion of the dough. Move your cupped hand in a quick, tight circular motion – this will cause the seam to come together and create tension on the surface of the dough and make the bun perfectly round. Repeat to shape all the buns, then place the buns on the lined baking trays. Cover with a lightly dampened dish towel and leave to prove for 1–1½ hours, depending on the room temperature, until doubled in size.

Towards the end of the proving time, preheat the oven to 190°C fan (410°C), gas 6.

Have ready a small pastry tamper or glass measuring 4cm (1½ inches) in diameter at the base. Sprinkle a little flour on the centre of a bun so that the tamper doesn't stick. Dip the tamper in flour, shaking off the excess, and use it to make an indentation in the centre of the bun. Repeat to make an indentation in all the buns. Place 1–2 teaspoonfuls of the vanilla custard in the centre of each, pushing the spoon down so the filling is sitting in the dough nicely. Bake for 12–14 minutes, or until golden. Leave to cool on a wire rack.

To coat the buns, mix the icing sugar and water to a thick paste. In a shallow pan, over a medium heat, toast one-third of the coconut until golden, stirring occasionally. Mix the toasted coconut with the rest of the coconut in a shallow bowl. Brush each bun with the icing, then heavily sprinkle with the coconut. Best eaten on the day of baking.

SEMLOR

Semlor usually appear in Swedish bakeries shortly after Christmas, but they are traditionally eaten on Shrove Tuesday, known as *Fettisdagen.* Swedes polish off a considerable number of these inviting cream buns on that day. Word has got out; they're now a regular feature in British bakeries, too. I like roasting the almonds in the filling, as this adds so much flavour. A piping bag is useful for this recipe.

MAKES 10 BUNS | **VO** (see page 153)

1 recipe quantity Tangzhong Method Dough (see page 34), with 1½ tbsp freshly ground cardamom added to the flour at step 2
strong white bread flour, for dusting
2–4 tbsp milk
icing (confectioners') sugar, for dusting

ROASTED ALMOND PASTE
130g (4¾oz) whole skin-on almonds
85g (3oz) caster (granulated) sugar

EGG WASH
1 large egg
1 tsp water
a pinch of fine sea salt

WHIPPED CREAM
500g (17oz) double (heavy) cream
1–2 tsp Vanilla Sugar (see page 150)

Recipe continues overleaf

Begin with the roasted almond paste: preheat the oven to 175°C fan (385°C), gas 5. Place the almonds on a baking tray and roast in the centre of the oven for 8–10 minutes, then leave to cool. Now pulse 110g (3¾oz) of the almonds in a food processor until they come together into a paste – you may have to add a tablespoon of water. Tip into a bowl and add the sugar. Chop the remaining nuts coarsely and add to the paste. Stir to distribute the chopped nuts evenly. Spoon into a container with a lid and place in the fridge until needed.

Line two baking trays with baking paper.

Knock back the dough and divide it into 10 equal pieces. To shape the buns, add a very small amount of flour to the work surface, then place your cupped hand over a portion of the dough. Move your cupped hand in a quick, tight circular motion – this will cause the seam to come together and create tension on the surface of the dough and make the bun perfectly round. Repeat to shape all the buns, then place the buns on the lined baking trays. Cover with a lightly dampened dish towel and leave to prove for 1–1½ hours, depending on the room temperature, until doubled in size.

Towards the end of the proving time, preheat the oven to 190°C fan (410°C), gas 6, and whisk together the ingredients for the egg wash.

Egg wash the buns and bake for 12–14 minutes, or until golden and sounding hollow when the undersides are tapped. Leave to cool on a wire rack.

Once the buns have cooled, they need to be hollowed out. Slice the top off of each bun, then scoop out a little of the insides. You're looking to remove about 5g (⅛oz) from each bun. Keep the crumbs.

Place the crumbs in a bowl with the almond paste. Now add 2 tablespoons of the milk and mix to form a paste. It should be a soft pipeable consistency, so you may have to add more milk.

Put the cream in a separate bowl and add the vanilla sugar to taste. Whip the cream until it just holds its form. Don't over whip as, once placed in a piping bag and piped, it will stiffen further. Transfer the cream to a piping bag fitted with a 15mm (½ inch) plain or star nozzle (or you can skip this step and just spoon the cream on).

Spoon the almond mixture into each bun. Pipe or spoon the cream on top, then place the tops back on. Dust with icing sugar and enjoy.

Eat on the day, or the day after baking. Store in a sealed plastic container in the fridge. Remove from the fridge 30 minutes before eating.

SPICED PEAR & PECAN

Rich and autumnal, this recipe is a great way to use up stale buns. It's a play on a Bostock, a name that doesn't sound very French, but likely originated as a way for bakeries to use up leftover brioche at the end of the day.

MAKES 10 BUNS | **VO** (see page 153)

10 plain stale buns (see tip below)
1 recipe quantity Frangipane (see page 51)
120g (4¼oz) pecans, chopped
icing (confectioners') sugar, for dusting

ROASTED PEARS
2 pears (about 300g/10½oz)
1 tbsp lemon juice

ALLSPICE SYRUP
2 tbsp golden caster (granulated) sugar
3 tbsp water
¼ tsp ground allspice
1 strip of pared lemon zest
1 tbsp maple syrup

TIP: This recipe calls for stale buns for filling, so the tangzhong method dough (see page 34) is perfect – just follow the recipe for any unfilled doughs.

For the pears, preheat the oven 180°C fan (400°C), gas 6. Peel and dice the pears and place in a bowl. Add the lemon juice and stir with a spoon. Lay out a sheet of foil on a baking tray and tip the pear pieces onto it. Now wrap the foil around the diced pear to make a parcel and bake for 25 minutes. Leave the pear wrapped in the foil to cool. Reduce the oven temperature to 165°C fan (370°F), gas 4.

To make the syrup, put the sugar, water, allspice and lemon zest in a small saucepan and add any juices from the cooked pears. Bring to a simmer, boil for a minute until the sugar has dissolved, then set aside to cool a little.

Line two baking trays with baking paper.

Slice a sliver from the top of a bun, then slice the bun in half, as you would a burger bun. Brush both cut sides with the allspice syrup, then place the bottom half of the bun on a lined baking tray. Spread a dessertspoon of frangipane on the bottom half of the bun. Now add some diced pear and chopped pecans and replace the top to make a bun sandwich. Spread a teaspoon of frangipane on the top of the bun, then add a few chopped nuts. Repeat to fill all the buns.

Bake for 22–25 minutes, or until the filling is cooked through. Remove from the oven and dust with icing sugar. Best eaten on the day of baking.

TOSCA BUNS

My mum made Tosca cake on many occasions when I was growing up. It's a great celebration cake – a featherlight sponge topped with almond caramel. The sweet, crunchy topping was the most appealing part to me. It was, and still is, my dad's favourite. This is essentially the same thing, in bun form. I've added white miso; it balances the sweetness and adds that lovely umami flavour. Pictured on pages 142–43.

MAKES 10 BUNS

1 recipe quantity Basic Enriched Dough (see page 26)
strong white bread flour, for dusting

MISO TOSCA TOPPING
40g ($1\frac{1}{2}$oz) unsalted butter
40g ($1\frac{1}{2}$oz) double (heavy) cream
40g ($1\frac{1}{2}$oz) icing (confectioners') sugar
$1\frac{1}{2}$ tbsp liquid glucose
1 tsp white miso paste
40g ($1\frac{1}{2}$oz) flaked (slivered) almonds

FILLING
85g (3oz) Almond Paste (see page 149)
65g ($2\frac{1}{4}$oz) unsalted butter

EGG WASH
1 large egg
1 tsp water
a pinch of fine sea salt

Begin with the Tosca topping: put the butter, cream, icing sugar and glucose in a small saucepan and bring to a slow boil. Add the miso and stir briskly. Continue boiling over medium heat, stirring occasionally, until it becomes a light brown caramel (approximately 8 minutes), then stir in the almonds. Using a teaspoon, spoon 10 mounds onto a baking tray lined with baking paper and set aside to cool.

To make the filling, crumble the almond paste into a bowl, add the butter and whisk until smooth and creamy. Set aside.

Line two baking trays with baking paper.

Knock back the dough. On a lightly floured work surface, roll out the dough to a rectangle measuring approximately 54 x 30cm (20¾ x 12 inches), lifting it a few times during rolling to release the tension in the dough. Spread the almond filling evenly over the dough with an offset spatula. With a short edge towards you, fold the dough in three, folding the bottom third up to cover the middle and the top third down to cover that. Gently roll out the dough again to a rectangle measuring 17 x 35cm (6½ x 14 inches).

With a pizza roller or a large knife, cut the dough into 10 strips along a short edge, each roughly 3½cm (1½ inches) wide. Cut along the length of a strip through the middle, almost to the top (it should look like a pair of trousers). Now twist the two strands of dough in different directions, twisting one clockwise and the other anti-clockwise, then tie them in a knot. Place on the lined baking trays and repeat to shape the remaining buns. Cover with a lightly dampened dish towel and leave to prove for 1–1½ hours, or until the dough springs back when you gently press it with your finger.

Towards the end of the proving time, preheat the oven to 190°C fan (410°C), gas 6, and whisk together the ingredients for the egg wash.

Egg wash the buns, then place a mound of miso Tosca topping on top of each bun.

Bake the buns for 10–12 minutes, or until golden. As the buns bake, the topping will melt, and some may slide off the bun. As soon as they come out of the oven, scoop up any topping that's on the baking tray and place back on the buns, taking care as the caramel will be very hot. Best eaten on the day of baking.

WHITE CHOCOLATE & PASSION FRUIT

The little passion fruit, with its craggy, wrinkled exterior, hides a delicious surprise within: golden pulp bursting with sweet, sour and juicy seeds. It complements rich, sweet and creamy white chocolate so well. A piping bag is useful for this recipe. Pictured on pages 146–47.

MAKES 10 BUNS

1 recipe quantity Tangzhong Method Dough (see page 34)
strong white bread flour, for dusting

WHITE CHOCOLATE FILLING
115g (4oz) white chocolate
120g (4¼oz) double (heavy) cream
140g (5oz) full-fat cream cheese
finely grated zest of ½ lemon

EGG WASH
1 large egg
1 tsp water
a pinch of fine sea salt

PASSION FRUIT TOPPING
3 passion fruit
2 tsp lemon juice
2 tsp golden caster (granulated) sugar

Begin with the white chocolate filling: melt the chocolate in a small heatproof bowl over a pan of simmering water, then remove from the heat. Set aside to cool for 5 minutes.

Whip the cream to soft peaks. In a separate bowl, lightly whisk the cream cheese with the lemon zest. Fold the cream into the cream cheese. Now add a tablespoon of the cream cheese mixture to the chocolate. It will stiffen immediately, but keep stirring. Now add another tablespoon and stir to incorporate. Follow with the remainder, folding to bring everything together. Cover and place in the fridge until needed.

Line two baking trays with baking paper.

Knock back the dough and divide it into 10 equal pieces. To shape the buns, add a very small amount of flour to the work surface, then place your cupped hand over a portion of the dough. Move your cupped hand in a quick, tight circular motion – this will cause the seam to come together and create tension on the surface of the dough and make the bun perfectly round. Repeat to shape all the buns, then place them on the lined baking trays. Cover with a lightly dampened dish towel and leave to prove for 1–1½ hours, depending on the room temperature, until doubled in size.

Towards the end of the proving time, preheat the oven to 190°C fan (410°C), gas 6, and whisk together the ingredients for the egg wash.

Egg wash the buns and bake for 12–14 minutes, or until golden and sounding hollow when the undersides are tapped. Leave to cool on a wire rack.

For the passion fruit topping, cut the passion fruits in half and scoop out the seeds into a small saucepan. Add the lemon juice and sugar. Bring to a simmer, cook for 1–2 minutes until syrupy, then remove from the heat. Pour into a small bowl, cover and set aside to cool.

Cut a hole at the top of each bun, a little wider than 1cm (½ inch), and hollow out a little of the crumb. Spoon the white chocolate filling into a piping bag fitted with a 1cm (½ inch) round nozzle. Pipe the filling into each bun, finishing with a swirl on the top. Make an indentation in the white chocolate filling with a warm teaspoon. Now add a teaspoonful of passion fruit filling to the centre of each bun. They are at their best on the day of baking.

TIP: These are also delicious with 1½ tablespoons of freshly ground cardamom added to the dough.

SUGAR SYRUP

Here are a handful of simple recipes that are handy for baking buns.

This simple sugar syrup is a liquid mixture made from equal parts water and sugar. It's a key ingredient that adds a lovely gloss and sweetness to baked goods. If you prefer less sweetness, you can omit it.

MAKES ENOUGH FOR BRUSHING 10 BUNS

25g (1oz) golden caster (granulated) sugar
25g (1oz) water

Put the sugar and water in a small saucepan and stir until the sugar is fully dissolved. Simmer for 1–2 minutes, without stirring.

Remove from the heat and leave to cool to room temperature. Store in an airtight container in the fridge for up to 4 weeks.

ALMOND PASTE

This differs from marzipan, as it contains less sugar. As well as for buns, it can be used in almond croissants or included in cake batters, cookie recipes and galettes. The addition of almond extract is optional.

MAKES 200g (7oz)

100g (3½oz) blanched almonds
100g (3½oz) icing (confectioners') sugar
20g (½oz) egg white or aquafaba
a few drops of natural almond extract (optional)

Put the almonds in a food processor and blitz until you have a fine meal. Add the icing sugar and egg white or aquafaba. Blitz again until it becomes a smooth paste. Add the almond extract, if desired. Store in an airtight container in the fridge for up to 4 weeks.

VEGAN 'EGG' WASH

MAKES ENOUGH FOR BRUSHING 10 BUNS

25g (1oz) soya or oat milk
10g (1¼oz) aquafaba
10g (1¼oz) maple or agave syrup

Blend all the ingredients. Store in an airtight container in the fridge for up to 5 days.

VANILLA SUGAR

This is really simple to make. The flavour is not as intense as commercially produced vanilla extract or paste, but it adds a lovely subtle note.

MAKES 100g (3½oz)

1 vanilla pod (bean)
100g (3½oz) golden granulated sugar

Begin by splitting the vanilla pod in half lengthways. Put the split pod in an ovenproof dish and place in the oven at 60°C fan (140°F), gas ¼ (or as low as your oven will go), for 1–2 hours. Once the time is up, turn the oven off and leave the pod in there until the oven is completely cool.

Now break the pod into small pieces, then place in a small high-speed blender with the sugar and blitz for 30 seconds. Alternatively, use a pestle and mortar. Pass the sugar through a fine sieve to remove any larger pieces. Store in an airtight container or jar in the fridge for up to 3 months.

VANILLA CUSTARD

There's nothing quite like homemade vanilla custard, especially when made with vanilla sugar for a deeper, more aromatic flavour.

MAKES 450g (1lb)

250g (9oz) full-fat milk
3 egg yolks (about 55–60g/2oz)
40g (1½oz) caster (granulated) sugar
1 tbsp Vanilla Sugar (see left)
15g (½oz) cornflour (cornstarch)
12g (½oz) unsalted butter

Pour the milk into a saucepan and set over a low heat. In a separate bowl, beat together the egg yolks, sugar, vanilla sugar and cornflour until pale and fluffy.

When the milk has come to a simmer, pour it over the egg mixture, whisking as you pour. Add the mixture back into the saucepan and bring this to a simmer, beating continuously. Continue to beat for 1–2 minutes, on a medium–low heat – the mixture will thicken rapidly. Once thickened, pour the custard into a clean bowl, add the butter and stir to combine. Place a piece of baking paper directly on the surface of the custard to stop a skin forming, and leave to cool completely before using. Best made a day ahead and stored in the fridge.

HOW TO MAKE VEGAN-FRIENDLY BUNS

Below is a list of simple swaps that can be made to a few ingredients, either using the vegan-friendly recipes provided or dairy-free alternatives, as noted.

APPLE & CINNAMON (SEE PAGE 48)
Use the Vegan Basic Enriched Dough (page 30) and Vegan 'Egg' Wash (page 149).

BUN WREATH (SEE PAGE 68)
Use the Vegan Basic Enriched Dough (page 30) and Vegan 'Egg' Wash (page 149).

CARDAMOM BUNS (SEE PAGE 73)
Use the Vegan Basic Enriched Dough (page 30) and Vegan 'Egg' Wash (page 149). Use dairy-free butter.

CLASSIC CHELSEA BUNS (SEE PAGE 74)
Use the Vegan Tangzhong Method Dough (page 38). Use dairy-free butter and replace the honey with maple syrup.

CHOCOLATE & TAHINI (SEE PAGE 78)
Use the Vegan Basic Enriched Dough (page 30) and Vegan 'Egg' Wash (page 149). Use dairy-free butter. Ensure the dark chocolate is vegan-friendly.

EARL GREY HOT CROSS BUNS (SEE PAGE 85)
Use the Vegan Tangzhong Method Dough (page 38). Use dairy-free milk.

FESTIVE SPICED BUNS (SEE PAGE 92)
Use the Vegan Basic Enriched Dough (page 30) and Vegan 'Egg' Wash (page 149). Use dairy-free butter.

HAZELNUT BUTTER & DATE (SEE PAGE 94)
Use the Vegan Basic Enriched Dough (page 30) and Vegan 'Egg' Wash (page 149).

NORDIC CINNAMON BUNS (SEE PAGE 106)
Use the Vegan Basic Enriched Dough (page 30) and Vegan 'Egg' Wash (page 149). Use dairy-free butter.

PISTACHIO, LIME & ROSE (SEE PAGE 116)
Use the Vegan Basic Enriched Dough (page 30) and Vegan 'Egg' Wash (page 149). Use dairy-free butter.

RASPBERRY & HIBISCUS (SEE PAGE 124)
Use the Vegan Basic Enriched Dough (page 30) and Vegan 'Egg' Wash (page 149).

SAFFRON, ALMOND & ORANGE (SEE PAGE 131)
Use the Vegan Basic Enriched Dough (page 30) and Vegan 'Egg' Wash (page 149). Use dairy-free butter.

SEMLOR (SEE PAGE 135)
Use the Vegan Tangzhong Method Dough (page 38) and Vegan 'Egg' Wash (page 149). Use dairy-free whipping cream.

SPICED PEAR & PECAN (SEE PAGE 138)
Use the Vegan Tangzhong Method Dough (page 38) and Vegan 'Egg' Wash (page 149).